Letters for Micah

❧ Letters for Micah

Navigating the Internal Dynamics of Your First Ministry

Leslie T. Hardin

WIPP & STOCK · Eugene, Oregon

LETTERS FOR MICAH
Navigating the Internal Dynamics of Your First Ministry

ISBN 13: 978-1-55635-726-8

Manufactured in the U.S.A.

For Micah

❧ Contents

﹖ Introduction

I've always found books of letters enjoyable reading. Rather than fleshing out your run-of-the-mill outline, letters contain personality, feeling, depth of insight into both the mind of the author and that of the recipient. In short, letters have an innate ability to carry the reader straight into the heart of the conversation.

The best of the classic devotional literature throughout Christian history can be found in booklets and collections of letters written from spiritual directors to their apprentices. Francois de Salignac de La Mothe-Fenelon (known simply as Fenelon) wrote arguably some of the best spiritual advice of the mid-seventeenth century. His works were compilations of advice that he had given to those under his care—first to the eight daughters of the Duc de Beauvilleiers, and later to the Duc of Burgundy (who was to succeed Louis XIV to the French throne). About the same time, Nicolas Herman (known to us as Brother Lawrence) articulated a series of conversations about living daily in the presence of the Almighty. His classic, *The Practice of the Presence of God*,[1] is replete with wisdom concerning the practice of spirituality in every-day living. Closer to our own time C. S. Lewis attracted wide attention with *The Screwtape Letters*[2] (though from a variegated perspective), and Dietrich Bonhoeffer's *Letters and Papers from Prison*[3] demonstrates the kind of clarity and faithfulness under trial that all Christians desire to emulate. The literature is wide and diverse in this area, and yet I must agree with Henri Nouwen, "It remains remarkable how little is said and written about letter writing as an important form of ministry."[4]

1. Lawrence, *The Practice of the Presence of God*.
2. Lewis, *The Screwtape Letters*.
3. Bonhoeffer, *Letters and Papers from Prison*.
4. Henri Nouwen, *The Genesee Diary*, 88.

I wrote this book in 2003 after reading Eugene Peterson's *The Wisdom of Each Other.*[5] His short collection of letters deals mainly with the topic of spiritual formation, its definition, and its implementation into daily living. I was fascinated with his approach and began thinking what possibilities existed for a book of this format in the area of ministry. I also noticed, as Nouwen said, that not much has been offered in this format. Ministry books are predominately deductive and focus primarily on the nuts and bolts of ministry. (While I was struggling to get this book into print Eerdmans published Michael Jinkins' book *Letters to New Pastors.*[6] His approach is much the same as mine, with more lengthy correspondence.)

What I offer here is a different approach, an approach that allows the reader to enter into the conversation between a seasoned pastoral veteran and an apprentice who leans on him for guidance in the difficulties of ministry. This collection is not solely about ministry. It attempts to bridge the gap between practical ministry and spiritual formation. You'll find some items here on praxis and technique. But I think the valuable contribution here involves the content which places ministry squarely on the shoulders of the spiritual foundation of the minister.

Acknowledgement must be given to Lyle Bundy, Professor of Counseling at Florida Christian College. Lyle adopted this text for his class, "Models of Leadership," and gave me the opportunity to share some of these ideas with the class. His request to use this as a textbook has been the main impetus to continue pursuing publication of this manuscript. Wipf and Stock was kind enough to take a chance on the project and put it into print, and for that, I am extremely grateful. Thirteen others also deserve mention. When I first formulated the idea and structure for this book, I thought it would be helpful to field-test the ideas with students who were training for ministry or heading in that direction. I solicited the involvement of thirteen people and e-mailed one chapter a week for an entire year, asking for their feedback on whether or not these ideas were hitting home for people training for ministry. Among them were students enrolled in my college classes and students considering ministry after high school: Jeff Crawford, Tony Galietti, Rob McGilvrey,

5. Peterson, *The Wisdom of Each Other.*

6. Jinkins, *Letters to Young Pastors.*

Jason Morrissey, James Reeves, Julie Reeves, Tony Robinson, Dave Rubarth, Jay Scott, Jason Taggert, Eric Templeton, and Kristie Wideen. The thirteenth person to read the original manuscript was Chris Ferguson, an Elder at Gateway Church of Christ (St. Albans, WV) and one of my best friends. I was writing as an ordained minister to prospective ministry candidates, and Chris was able to provide feedback from a third angle, that of the local church elder. He helped shed light on issues lurking in the shadows.

Some of the letters contained here are actual correspondence I exchanged with young people facing problems in ministry. As I looked to include them, I needed to protect the names of those to whom the letters were sent. I chose to address each of the letters to a young man named Micah. It was the best idea I could come up with at the time, and none of the people involved in any of the letters/e-mails shared this name. I have a son named Micah, and while it was not for him that this book was written, I pray that he will gain wisdom from it when he considers God's calling on his life. If I've done my job correctly, the wisdom here will last long after I'm gone.

Looking forward,

Les Hardin
November 2007

ॐ Why Ministry?

Micah,

I can't tell you how ecstatic I am that you've decided to enter the ministry! I sensed the Lord was growing deep within you, and I'm excited that He's put within your heart a desire for ministry within the Kingdom.

If you'll permit me, I'd like to offer you two cautions about the perception of ministry. The way we think about something affects the way we act on it, and I'd like to caution you about these two extremes.

First, *don't think that ministry is a mundane profession.* This is a noble profession you're about to embark upon! As a minister of the Body of Christ, you have the opportunity to serve the living God in the midst of his people, to be a guide for them, to enlighten them about the transformation of the Spirit in their lives, and to work in partnership to advance the Kingdom of God every single day. Jesus was sold out to ministry during his time here, and we have the awesome privilege of following in his footsteps. To be sold out to God in such a way as to have your full-time devotion given to Him is indeed a privilege.

But don't think that ministry is the most elite profession in the world either. Earlier in my career, I believed that ministry in the Kingdom was the *most* elite profession, that it was the only profession which had eternal significance, and that members of the congregation ought to respect me for it. It was an arrogance sprung from my insecurity and it got me into trouble. To elevate myself in that regard communicated to everyone around me that what they did on an everyday basis had no eternal significance. That just isn't true! Every profession, every career, every job for the one who has professed faith in Christ has eternal significance. The doctor who runs his practice from the center of the heart of Christ knows that his operation may give this person one more day to live and one more chance to repent. The lawyer who has given his heart to Christ runs his practice in such a manner as to show the world how God works for justice in the world. The factory worker who can stand on the line and influence his co-workers regarding the integrity and honesty of Jesus has just as much eternal significance in his work than any full-time minister. Everything we do, not just full-time ministry, has eternal significance,

The joy of ministry is this: we get to work with the best people in the world. If Christ has done his work (and I think he has), and if the Spirit lives in His Body (and I think he does), then the people that we get to work with really are the best people in the world. Not because they are "good, moral people." Not because they're Americans. And certainly not because they are members of our churches! They're the best people in the world because Christ is alive in them! He motivates them to give massive amounts of their time, energy, and resources for the same reason you've given your vocation. The Spirit of the Almighty that we serve is alive and well in the hearts, minds and lives of those who have given themselves to Him. Sometimes they make mistakes. Sometimes they don't see the road ahead and make the wrong decisions. And sometimes they're just downright sinful. But ask yourself on a constant basis, "Am I ever any of those things?" I think you'll find yourself in the same situations more often than you care to admit.

৯ How to Know If Ministry's for You

Micah,

Greetings! It's so good to hear from you once again. I've kept in touch with your father over the years, and I'm familiar with what's going on in the church you regularly attend. But it's been a while since I've spoken with you and I'm glad to hear from you once again.

I hear that you're thinking about ministry, and that you'd like some advice from someone who's made ministry a vocation. My guess is that you have a desire for ministry, but you don't want to make a lifelong career decision without first considering whether this is the right direction for you. I understand your hesitancy, and I'm happy to offer some considerations.

If you're thinking about ministry because you have some inner desire to be liked and needed by others, ministry is not for you. Ministry in the local church certainly puts you in a position to be needed by others, but if you're responding from this deficiency in your life, you're in for some trouble down the road. Being needed certainly makes you feel important, but it can lead you to the point where your schedule is overrun with those who "need" you and can give you an inflated sense of ego. If you do this because you want to be liked by masses of people, I'd encourage you to think about your own personal insecurities and remind you that there will certainly be times in ministry when you will not be liked in the least.

If you're thinking about ministry because it seems easy, you're certainly in for some huge disappointment. The minister in today's congregations is required to be proficient at a number of things: administration, public speaking, classroom teaching, shepherding, leadership, counseling, conflict resolution, writing, visitation, crisis management, and the ever-elusive skill of saying the right thing at the right time. This is not an easy calling, and if you embark upon this because you think it's easy, I'd like to become a partner with your therapist, because he's going to make a lot of money!

(And if you're in this for the money, you're barking up the wrong tree. If that's your primary reason for considering ministry you'll do more harm to God's people than good.)

So what is the proper motivation for ministry? *Passion.* Passion for God—to serve him, to please him, to utilize your gifts for him. Passion for God's people—to see them growing into Christ-likeness, to help them take the next step on the journey, to give them a shoulder to cry on and a resource to consult in their spiritual journey. If you have a passion in these areas, if you desire to help others without regard for what it costs you (financially or otherwise) and if you have a passion to do what God has asked you to do for the rest of your life, then your motivations are headed in the right direction.

How do you know where your passion lies? Consider what you'd enjoy doing for the rest of your life, day in and day out, and you'll begin to understand your passion. My passion is teaching— teaching the Scriptures, mentoring young people for ministry in the Kingdom, and helping people take the next steps in their developing spirituality. My grandfather once offered me this advice: "Find something that you love to do and you'll never have to work a day in your life." When you are employed for your passion, it's not work, not just a job. It's what you love to do. Howard Thurman said, "Do not ask what the world needs. Ask what makes you come alive and go do it. Because what the world needs is people who have come alive." That's good advice for you. Consider what would keep you alive, passionate, and you'll have your answer. Your passion will sustain you through times of doubt, times of difficulty, times when your schedule is so busy you can't see to next week, and times when the next step is impossible to see.

I hope this helps. I'm curious to know how you'll work this out. Ultimately this is your decision, but I'm happy to help in any way I can.

3

❧ Seminary

Micah,

It's good to hear from you again. To be honest, I was surprised by your choice to attend Meadowbrook University. I thought you'd choose someplace closer to home. But the choice you've made is an excellent one, and you're sure to get a first-class education and training for ministry there.

I understand your previous question regarding the necessity of seminary. You are correct, none of the apostles went to seminary . . . at least not to a formal one. Your assumption is valid in factual content, but a bit naive in practical application. The difference between them and us is that they had the privilege of learning everything they needed to know about ministry in the Kingdom from the lips of Jesus himself. We don't have that privilege. We have the ability to know what Jesus said through the pages of Scripture, but we won't ever be able to sit at his feet and ask him questions and have him respond in that moment.

Seminary helps us understand what ministry is all about. As I said earlier, the way you think about something determines the way you act upon it. To act in ministry in a responsible fashion we must *think* about ministry responsibly, and seminary helps us do that. Greek and Hebrew, despite your consternation that these are requirements for your degree, help you come to terms with what is *actually* being said in the pages of Scripture. Biblical studies help you build a foundation for ministry. Courses in the social sciences (psychology, sociology, and counseling) help you understand why people behave the way they do in certain situations. The humanities bring you to terms with the evolving world culture, and the practical ministries work you'll do helps you bring all of that thinking into a methodical approach to ministry based on your thoughtful foundations. Your seminary studies help you to think about what you're doing so that you can approach ministry with a purposeful intent.

Let me also caution you that these years you spend in seminary will form habits in you that will remain longer than you intend. If you spend all your time in study during these years and never any time developing other aspects of your spirituality, then you'll approach ministry in your first congregation with the same proficiency at study and alienate those who express their spirituality through their hands and their emotions. Continue to exercise through these years so that you don't get out of shape. I went to seminary having been co-captain of the football team, an avid hunter, and had a physically strenuous job on the family farm. But nobody made me exercise in seminary, and I fell poorly out of shape. I'm finding now that it takes longer to undo through discipline what it took me only a couple of years to accomplish by sloth. Exercise relieves stress and helps you think clearly; it will be good for your study habits. Also, get into the habit of Sabbath, a day of rest. Just because your life is devoted to service doesn't mean that you don't need breaks every now and then. Your temptation will be to study during the week and to work on the weekends in the smaller churches. Utilize those opportunities, but find one day when you don't study or work. You'll be much more effective. I don't mean to tell you how to structure your life. These are the formative years, and I only want you to develop good habits that will last a lifetime.

I'm only a couple of hours away. If you need something, or would like to escape for the weekend, my home is always open to you. I'd love to sit and chat, spend some time with you. Perhaps I'll take you fishing in the stream behind my house. I find it a quiet place to listen to the Lord and work out my own issues. It's a holy place for me these days.

❧ The First Ministry Opportunity

Micah,

I was happy to receive your e-mail yesterday. It's been a while since we've been in touch, but I've kept up with your studies and your life through a couple of my friends who teach at Meadowbrook. I'm glad to know that your studies are going well.

I've looked over the stuff that you sent me from the High Point church. I think that your intention to be involved in a weekend ministry is the right thing to do, but in my opinion and discernment, this is neither the church nor the time for you. In the first place, High Point says that they are seeking a weekend Youth Minister, and my guess is that this is what you thought you would sign up for. But as I look over the job description they've sent to you, and considering your comments to me yesterday about the expectations revealed to you in the interview, they're asking you for much more than you can possibly handle. They've said they want your involvement to only be 15 hours a week, but the job description involves work equivalent to a 40-hour a week ministry. They want you involved in Sunday School first hour, Children's Church second hour, High School Youth Group on Sunday night, and visitation and events on Saturdays. All of these are normal for a weekend assignment of this sort. I also hear you saying that they want you to utilize your talent in music (which I hear is quite extraordinary) to participate in worship on Sunday mornings, and to attempt to help build a Wednesday night program. I realize you're only 30 minutes away from High Point, but nobody can do what they are asking in 15–20 hours a week. I suspect that, sensing you are passionate about getting started in ministry, they feel they can exploit your passion by paying you for only 15–20 hours a week and hope that you'll give them the rest for free. It's not the free stuff

I mind. Every minister who's passionate about his work goes above and beyond the call of duty. What bothers me is the underhanded nature I perceive in trying to exploit your inexperience.

But that's not the only reason I suggest you turn this opportunity down. Your incessant whining to me in our last exchange about the amount of work you have to do this year for your studies is a red flag that you need not enter any ministry situation at this time. On the reading of books . . . stop complaining to me and read! In the time you typed out that lengthy e-mail you could have read three chapters of any of those texts. You won't get any sympathy from me either. I'm a voracious reader and it's my opinion that the more input you have about ministry, about the Scriptures, and about the world in general, the better prepared you are for ministry. Until you realize that, you're not ready for the responsibility of the influence you'll have over others in the Kingdom. You'll only wind up communicating by your attitude and your lifestyle that the Christian life involves little work.

Not to worry. This is normal at this stage in your life. Meadowbrook has ceased to become the glamorous, adult-version of church camp that you idolized and has brought you face to face with your own lack of self-discipline. It happens to most people in this year. Distance yourself from the complaining of your dorm mates on this issue and you'll get through it a lot easier. (Most of my friends who constantly complained about their workloads are no longer in ministry.) Perhaps this will help. With every assignment, ask yourself, "How will this prepare me for ministry?" Even if it's as simple as forcing you to do something you'd rather not do, that's a valuable training tool. Every action, every assignment, every book you read, every class you attend is a test of character. If you won't do what is asked of you, your ministry is ruined from this moment. If you can get yourself to embrace the things that people are asking you to do and do them in timely fashion, you'll set yourself up for integrity and dependability in every aspect of ministry.

5

❧ Negotiating Salary

Micah,

I think it's a wise thing to be applying for ministry positions this early in your final season at Meadowbrook. Most students in your position wait until the spring, and to be fair, that's when most churches know that students are looking. But your experiences and your background (in my humble opinion) put you in a class above most of your peers, and you'd be a fine addition to any church staff. (Don't let that go to your head, now!) Getting a start on it now gets your name out there as a serious candidate and shows that you have foresight and the ability to make decisions well in advance of the deadlines. That will speak volumes to any search committee.

You had asked me whether it was appropriate for you to be negotiating salary at this stage in your career. I think it's wise that you're thinking about this ahead of time. Most people (not just your age, either) go into the interview with no consideration as to what they'll come and work for, what perks they want from the job, and what adequate compensation this ministry properly entitles them to. I made this mistake once. I went into the interview not expecting to negotiate salary. I thought the purpose of the interview was to consider whether I was a good fit for this congregation and whether they wanted me to come and serve with them. Toward the end of the interview the chairperson of the committee said, "Okay, now you're going to accompany Mr. So and So and negotiate what it will take to bring you here." He had done his homework on what I was already making and had the upper hand. I wish I had been prepared in that moment to detail my desire in a more articulate fashion.

A good rule of thumb in your situation is to consider what public educators with similar degrees are making in the community.

If you're applying for a youth ministry position, call the community's school board or the state Department of Education and find out what the local High School teacher makes in your community. If it's a preaching ministry, call the local community college and inquire about those who spend their life teaching adults. You might even want to find out how other churches in the area are compensating their ministers. In this situation, knowledge is power, and the more you know the better equipped you'll be. (This isn't limited to monetary compensation either. Consider in your research what other perks are given to people in the community—health insurance, disability, vacation time, retirement contributions, professional education and development, etc.)

I understand that this can be construed as treating ministry like a business. I can hear some of the elders in one of the churches I served saying, "Ministry is servant-hood. How dare you treat it with the aggressive tactics of the business world to acquire more wealth for yourself?" And the simple answer to that is that some churches want you to come and serve for pennies and not compensate you adequately at all. Some churches see it as their mission to keep their ministers humble through their minuscule compensation. It's a sort of ecclesiastical pride that belittles both congregation and minister, and sends the wrong message to the community. It shows that they don't take the work of ministry seriously. Both Jesus and Paul affirm that "the worker is worth his wages" (Luke 10:7; 1 Tim. 5:18). In some denominational settings the salaries are set and negotiation is not necessary. But in our non-denominational scenario, without a centralized headquarters to tell us what to pay whom, we have to do this independently.

Now with that said, let me also tell you that my practice over the years has been to negotiate in the beginning, but *never* afterward. "Be content with your pay" (Luke 3:14). In the beginning, it shows that you are serious about the job and about what the Lord has called you to do. When you keep negotiating after you've arrived, it belittles the work you're doing and sets you apart as one who's greedy.

Money can become a stumbling block for both congregation and minister if these things aren't handled honestly and delicately. Do your best to know your parameters before you interview, and stick to them. When both church and candidate are comfortable in this area, then you'll have a great basis to know how your relationship will progress in other areas outside the arena of financial compensation.

6

❧ Interview Questions

Micah,

I'm sorry this has taken so long to get to you, but it took me some time to think about it. Here are some of the questions I'd be concerned about asking during the interview. Keep in mind that this list isn't complete, and you certainly won't want to ask *all* of these questions during the interview. But they'll serve as a resource for you. Enjoy!

Interview Questions

1. What is the average tenure of ministers at this church over the past twenty years?

2. Why did the previous minister in this position leave?

3. In one word, how would you describe the staff relationships here?

4. Describe the financial stability of this congregation over the past twenty years.

5. What is this congregation's greatest asset?

6. What does this congregation do better than any other church in the community?

7. What does this congregation do that nobody else is thinking of?

8. Describe this congregation's greatest weakness.

9. What steps have been taken in the last three years to overcome those weaknesses?

10. What is this congregation's big "secret?" (*It's my experience that every congregation has something they'd rather you not know until you've worked there three years. See if they'll tell you now.)

11. What expectations do you have of my family?

12. In general, how would you describe the relationships amongst members of the congregation?

13. If I take this job, what will be my greatest obstacle to success?

14. Who will be my number one supporter?

15. Who is the person that I should get on board first if I am to succeed?

16. Who is the person who will be my most vocal challenger?

17. Share with me this congregation's mission statement, values, purpose and vision.

18. What goals does the leadership of this congregation have in regard to those values and vision?

19. How do you plan to achieve those goals?

20. How do you expect me to contribute to the purpose, vision, and achievement of those goals?

21. How do you deal with disciplinary situations amongst the staff?

22. How do you deal with disciplinary situations amongst the membership?

23. Will I have the freedom to develop new paradigms and programs? Or will I be expected to work from pre-determined templates?

24. What freedom do I have to be involved in Kingdom work outside the context of this congregation?

25. Do I have the freedom to set and manage my own schedule? Or is that determined for me?

26. Is there a budget delineated for the job I'm interviewing for? (Ask to see it.)

27. What is the relationship between Elders, Deacons and Staff here?

28. What is the Eldership required/expected to be involved in?

29. What is the Deaconship required/expected to be involved in?

30. What is the role of each of the staff to be?

31. Who is the person to whom I am accountable in this position?

32. Are there any other people to whom I am accountable?

33. Tell me how you go about supporting your staff in times of crisis?

34. Are there any projects, programs or special events that you're expecting me to be involved in that are not written in the job description?

35. How do you go about evaluating your staff to determine effectiveness?

36. What is the cost of living like in this area?

37. As you look at my resume and my background, what concerns do you have? How can I help to alleviate those concerns?

38. Describe the compensation package for me.

39. And be sure to ask about holidays, vacation time, and days off.

My one piece of advice is that you get as many answers as you need to make an informed decision about this job. You'll want to exercise *some* discretion as to how many questions you ask, but as a general rule, search committees won't be offended by too many questions. It signals that you've done your homework.

7

৯ Unwritten Expectations

Micah,

As you're interviewing, also be sure to inquire about the unwritten expectations that will be thrust upon you in your ministry. It's difficult to get this information from the Search Committee, or even from the Leadership. There will most certainly be a written job description, but you will also, over the course of time, be asked to do certain things that are not a part of your job description.

There are two ways to think about this. The first says, "Well, if it's not part of my job description, then I won't do it." That's irresponsible and has little integrity. In the course of ministry things come up that need doing, and if you're the one most gifted to attack the issue, then by all means, you should go for it. Everyone has certain duties and aspects of their job that they don't like that must be performed. It's part of being a contributor. Most who do only what they want to do and refuse to do anything else quickly find themselves unemployed.

The second way to think about this is to remind yourself that you'll be asking permission at some point in your ministry to engage in areas of service that are not part of your job description. Let's say you've been hired as a Minister of Education, but you want to use your musical talents to lead one of the primary worship bands. You'd be less than happy if the leadership said to you, "That's not part of your job description." So recognize that there is some latitude on both sides of this job description. It's been my experience that the "job description" serves as a guide, and if either you or the leadership of the congregation has to go consulting (and enforcing) the job description, you've got problems.

Nevertheless, there are always those unwritten expectations, the activities that will be thrust upon you that no one will communicate to you until it's too late. I once went to a congregation as a Youth Minister, only to have the Senior Minister say to me, "Oh, by the way, the Youth Minister is always in charge of the Christmas Eve service. I'll be on vacation during Christmas." I was flabbergasted!

How do you find out what the unwritten expectations are? That's a good question. I'd suggest that you begin by asking the Search Committee or the leadership team directly what those things are. If you don't get the answers you're looking for, you might also try contacting former ministers of the congregation. They'd be in the best position to answer your questions.

Don't get bogged down with this, and don't make it the focus of the interviews. You'll need some defense mechanisms to deal with these unwritten expectations, but they shouldn't be stringent or violently reactionary. Just keep this in mind as you're interviewing and recognize that this is a vital component of the information you'll need to make an intelligent decision as to whether or not you should pursue this relationship further.

8

æ The First Five People

Micah,

I'm excited to hear that you've taken the Associate Minister's position at the Oriole Street Church. You'll enjoy it, and you'll be an asset to their approach to ministry. I know they want you there as soon as possible, but I think it's wise that you're taking some significant time to pray about this new ministry before you go.

I want to tell you something that may be controversial, and may sound insensitive at first, but hear me out. A gentleman experienced in ministry gave me this advice once, and though it was a bit shocking at first, I quickly learned of his wisdom and want to share that with you now.

Beware of the first five people who seek you out in any new ministry.

Now that it's out there, let me explain. When you approach this new ministry situation there will be a handful of people (not necessarily five) who will seek you out and clamor for your attention from the moment you arrive. Chances are, they want something from you. They will seek you out because they want to get to you *first*, before anybody else can. And the reason they want your attention *first* is that they haven't been able to gain support for their ideas, opinions or programs through the leadership of the church. They hope that by getting to you first that you will side with them and implement their ideas for them. In their minds they hope you'll be the champion they haven't found in the leadership thus far.

There's a reason that the leadership hasn't responded favorably. Be sensitive to that. And know that the leaders in the Oriole Street Church will be standing back watching you deal with these situations. Those who seek your attention first will be those who feel

17

a sense of urgency. You may be, in their minds, the last hope for their rejected ideas. Those who know that they will have a long-term relationship with you (even long-term influence upon your ministry) will be content to wait their turn. They're secure in that long-term influence.

I make it a habit when we hire a new staff person to keep my distance for the initial period. I know that long-term I'll have a greater influence on this person's thinking, programming and ministry because of the every-day nature of staff relationships than any of the people who are desperately trying to get this person's attention in the first two weeks. I'll be their most avid supporter in the long-run, and those who have come and gone here will attest to my support.

I've also found this scenario to be true in my own ministries. I've served three churches now, and I can recall the first five people to seek my involvement in each location. In each case, every person in that group was either one of my biggest frustrations in ministry or had left the church within my first year.

That's not to say that you need to give the cold shoulder to the first people you meet. I'm not saying that at all. Most who fall into this pattern are not cognizant of their actions or their effects in this matter. A few will be genuine. They're honestly glad to have you on board and are anticipating your arrival. Those folks honestly want to help you in any way possible. I just want you to be aware of the pattern that I've seen in every new ministry I've begun.

May God bless you in this new ministry, Micah! I'm privileged to be involved with you in this way, and count it a blessing from the Lord to be an encouragement to you as you serve Him.

9

❧ Your First Week on the Job

Micah,

I'm glad to hear that your first week on the job is going well. It's always an exciting time to meet new people, explore your newfound ministry context, and to imagine the possibilities of what this new adventure holds for the ministry of Christ in the world.

I also sense your frustration at not knowing what to do during this first week. That's normal. I had a roommate in college who, after his first week in full-time ministry, said to me, "I sat around for three days wondering what I was supposed to be doing! I felt so guilty." I didn't understand what he meant until I took my first full-time ministry position . . . and sat around for three days wondering what I was supposed to be doing! It's happened in all three locations I've served in ministry. That first week is difficult, but you'll get rolling on it soon enough. As you get to know the people involved in this ministry you'll quickly see where the work needs to be done and how to best accomplish the goals you've set for your ministry there. Eventually, because I know you to be the kind of person who's self-motivated, you'll develop too many ideas and programs to legitimately and adequately be accomplished by any one person in ministry, or that can even be accomplished in one place.

All of this is normal. Every minister faces this situation during the first week (or two) in ministry. It's not supposed to stay this way. It should pass, and quickly. But for now, it's normal. Meanwhile, use this time wisely. Be prepared for your teaching opportunities and meetings, and demonstrate to this community of faith your level of intensity in every endeavor.

10

❧ No Changes the First Six Months!

Micah,

If I understand you correctly, your question is, "What pace of change is appropriate for the congregation with a new minister?" Your question is a curious one. Change is difficult for any age group. Less so for younger generations, but difficult for everyone. So when you ask me, "How soon should I go about making needed changes to the programming here?" you have to keep in mind that it's not an easy question. Here are the things I would consider.

First, I'd consider the history of the congregation in this area. Does the congregation have a history of ministers who made sweeping changes in their first six months and then didn't stay long? Does the history reflect that no changes have ever been made by new ministers? History can make all the difference. For instance, I once knew a youth minister who was required to hand in his lesson plans for all classes he taught to be approved by the Elders of the congregation. He was desperate about changing this, but my counsel to him was that if he dug into the history of the youth ministers who had gone before him, he would probably find that some of his predecessors had been either teaching false doctrine or addressing issues inappropriate for that particular age group. It seemed as if the Elders were trying to prevent this from happening again. He dug around a bit and found that his immediate predecessor had, in fact, been doing both and was dismissed for refusing to cooperate with the Eldership on this matter. For the young man I was counseling, my advice was simply, "Turn them in. Don't complain about it. Just turn them in. And make them top-notch from the first lesson plan." He was paying the price for the sins of those who had gone before him and his only recourse in eradicating this watchdog type of accountability was to prove to them from the outset that he wasn't the kind of person who needed to be held on a leash. History makes all the difference.

How do you find this out? Get into the church paper (if they have one) and read the last ten year's worth. Ask some of the members who have been around a long time what their perception is of change and new ministry positions. It will take some time, but if you'll look for the corroboration in various testimonies you'll find the thread of opinion that underlies the change climate in the Oriole Street Church.

Second, you'll want to consider the people involved. I know this is difficult right now, but you'll want to ask yourself, "Who are the major players in this ministry change?" Whatever issue it is that you're considering making change on, discover who will be on your side and who will stand against this change. I hate to talk about comparing the opinions of people, but the simple fact is that if you have all of the leadership on board and a hand full of infrequent attendees who will oppose you, the answer is obvious.

Third, uncover the level of dissatisfaction surrounding the issue. There could very well be a healthy level of dissatisfaction in the matter, and the congregation might be waiting for someone with the nerve to take it on. If that's the case, you've got the green light for progressing with desired change. On the other hand, if you speak about the problem to ten people and nine of them didn't know the problem existed before your counsel, you'll want to wait. Making changes in line with the level of dissatisfaction can put you in a favorable light with this congregation.

Now, having said all of that, here's my golden nugget of advice in this matter: *don't make any major changes in the first six months.* I know that the common sentiment you receive at seminary is that you should make as many changes as possible during the first six months, because you might not get to make any more changes again. In my humble opinion, this is irresponsible leadership and can partially account for the high turnover rate and short tenure amongst your peers. Right now, these people are watching you to see if you will live up to the expectations that they have for you. Prove to them that you're not here to upset their apple cart. Live among them as a fellow pilgrim. Make changes *with* them, not *for* them. You're not a hired gun for these people. You're now a fellow worshiper with them, a member of their faith community, and a brother to whom they look for leadership. Treat that gift with great responsibility. I've met few people in the Kingdom who would not respect you for it. And with respect comes . . . the willingness to embrace change!

❧ The First Month Sets the Standard

Micah,

I'm excited that you're enjoying so much success early in your ministry there at the Oriole Street Church. Your early success in evangelism and teaching are contagious, no doubt, and will set the stage for your ministry for the next year. The first month makes a huge impression on the congregation. The church is looking to you (*at* you may be more appropriate!). And the old adage remains true: you never get a second chance to make a first impression. So impress them with your life and your work from the outset.

This is not new advice. Paul gave this counsel to a preacher as young as yourself when he told Timothy not to let those in Ephesus look down upon him because he was young. He didn't want Timothy to fall into the trap to which some of the people in the church there had expected him to succumb. Rather, he expected that Timothy would rise above it and embrace the challenge of "setting an example" or *impressing* these people with his speech, his lifestyle, the way he loved them in spite of conflict and disappointment, in his incredible faith in Christ Jesus, and his purity (1 Tim. 4:12).

These are all noteworthy goals for you as well. Show those around you that your speech is above the criticism and condemnation of those you disagree with and that you will not tolerate back-biting among the people with whom you have influence. Demonstrate to them the possibility of a life wholly committed to Jesus, proving that it's not for the ultra-spiritual but attainable by everyday people. You're bound to encounter some conflict, and when you do, show them your love for them at all costs. That doesn't mean that you won't be angry at times, but it's possible to love them in the midst of it. Be a person who reflects the purity that mirrors the life of Christ.

Satan has destroyed many a minister in this area, and your attention to it early will help prevent future embarrassment, for you and for Christ Jesus.

Early in ministry as you are, meditation and study of the Pastoral Letters (1–2 Timothy and Titus) can be extremely helpful. They're written to young ministers such as yourself and their counsel is invaluable for the novice.

❧ When You Want to Quit

Micah,

Feel free to vent to me anytime. I'm sorry that this is happening to you. I'm here for you, you know that. And you know that I care about you a great deal. Make no mistake about that. Every time I think about your being in ministry, it is an encouragement to me and a validation of my own ministry. You know how much I care for you, and how much I respect the work you're doing in order to hear what I have to say and not be upset with me.

You've been in this ministry for six weeks, and already you want to quit? This does not bode well for your ministry in any field, let alone youth ministry. *Every* new minister, *every* new ministry situation, *every* new job has its problems, its hassles and its trials. Don't think that just because you're in a youth ministry that things would be better for you if you got into a worship ministry position. Instead of fielding complaints from angry and self-righteous parents about why their kid isn't receiving as much attention as others, you'd be receiving complaints from angry and self-righteous people about the song selection, the inclusion of contemporary-style songs, and the fact that the lights were turned down too low. Believe me, I've been in both of the ministries you're talking about and you can trust me when I say that there are belligerent and self-righteous people in *any* ministry you begin. The first six months that I came to Walnut Street were *exactly* what you are describing to me.

You're correct to say that I taught you that it's wise to know your limitations. But if that's the only thing you learned from me then I'll be sorely disappointed. I hope that you've also learned from me that ministry is not for quitters, that leadership takes nerves of steel, and that the Lord's church is to be treated with the utmost respect. I hope that you also learned that ministry is servant-hood, a commitment to striving for excellence in the midst of everyday living. And I hope that you learned that ministry is *hard work*!

You and Rhonda will have to sit down and talk about the changing nature of your responsibilities and relationship. Until now you've had all of the time in the world to give her. That was bound to change whenever you entered the located ministry. So don't think that you can go back to the time when you could just pick her up and go wherever and do whatever. It was going to change sooner or later, and the sooner the better. I dated a girl once who couldn't handle the time I spent in ministry at East Union. She was jealous of my attention to those students. When I began to date Kara she also had the same troubles. But she was willing to work through them and came to realize that just because I didn't spend time with her on some occasions didn't mean that I didn't love her. We had to work that out early in our relationship. To be honest, the time thing still affects us. But you have to learn how to work through it.

On Tamara . . . love her. If she wants you gone, be the bigger man and don't let her bother you so much. Be the more spiritually mature person and gently win her over. It will take an iron will, and guts of steel. You'll have to endure some of her sorry comments. But ministry will never be free of people who get on your nerves. You might as well learn how to deal with it now and get on with your life. You may have to confront her about her negative attitude. That has its own set of rules, and you need not do that until you get some guidance on how to do so. It may come to that, and if so, it will be messy. I had to crawl up in Gary Reed's face a few weeks ago, and that was messy. But it had to be done. Broken bones must be re-set sometimes. It's very painful, but it's the only way to true healing and future use of the limb.

Leadership isn't easy. It takes inner strength, fortitude, and a commitment to your vision. Sometimes it's pain. But, as the Dread Pirate Roberts said to Princess Buttercup in *The Princess Bride*, "Life is pain, Princess, and anyone who tells you otherwise is trying to sell you something!"

Okay, I've said enough for today. Please don't take my harsh tone as a full reprimand. I don't mean it that way. I sense the Adversary landing on you and I'll not sit idly by and let him perpetrate his lies on you without a fight.

13

❧ The Crisis

Micah,

New insights hit me in the last day or two regarding your situation. You're in the Crisis. *Everybody* has this in the first stages of ministry. Initially you are excited about the possibilities. But when you get into the midst of everyday living and realize that it's much more difficult than you had imagined, you're faced with the possibility that your dreams for this place may never be realized. That's when you enter the Crisis. It's the time when you say (and tell me if this isn't exactly where you are), "What have I done? I should have never agreed to come here! This was the worst mistake I've ever made in my life!" I had the crisis in my first two weeks at East Union. I had the crisis after my first three months at Springfield. It took me a whole year to get over it here at Walnut Street. I kept saying to myself, "I just ran away from Springfield. I should have never come here. Walnut Street is *not* the place for me." But once you get past it you begin to realize that God has put you in this place for a purpose, and you wouldn't be here if God didn't have something in mind for you. When you took the job there at the Oriole Street Church, you had a particular vision for the ministry to which God called you. You're discouraged because you know that your plans will never come to fruition as you envisioned them. Now, at this point you have two options in regard to the realization of your dream. You can give up on it and quit (which is what the Adversary wants from you, in my opinion), or you can alter the vision and contextualize it for this specific ministry situation. You made dreams and plans based on a church you didn't know that well. Now that you have some more intimate knowledge of how it works and the problems involved, your dream will be more effective. But it will have to change to meet the needs of the people you now know.

Micah, if God thought that anybody else in the whole tri-state area could do the job as well as you could, *that* person would be working at the Oriole Street Church and not you. Think about your history and how you got to this point. It's an amazing story, and just because it's common to you doesn't mean that God's hand wasn't in it. Every event in your life (and especially the events of last summer) has led you to this place.

The rest is His-story. God clearly wants you in this place, and to forsake the calling at this point is to say to the Lord, "It's too hard and I can't do it." Moses said the same thing about getting Pharaoh to free the Hebrew slaves (Exod. 3:11, 4:1, 13). "It's too hard!" If you'll recall, the only thing God asked Moses to do was to deliver a message to Pharaoh: "Let my people go." God didn't ask Moses to free the slaves. That was God's business, accomplished through the plagues and the hardening of Pharaoh's heart. All Moses was asked to do was to deliver the message.

Be faithful to the task that God has appointed for you. Let him take care of the rest. The Eldership there is not ignorant of the struggles you're having with Thelma. I'd bet a month's salary on that. Chris, your partner in that ministry, is a member of the Clinkenbeard mob that is so prominent in that congregation, and he's married the prized daughter of the Chairman of the Elders. I guarantee you that Chris has informed them all of the way Thelma is treating you and they are not ignorant of it. They may simply want to see how you deal with it before they get involved. Impress them with your leadership skills!

Let me quote for you one more thing, this from the Desert Fathers. If any of the desert monks wanted to leave his group, if any of them was restless and bored, unable to see his purpose, if any of them believed they would find rest from their troubles in another place, they would have surely benefited from this counsel from Abba Moses. One of the most revered of the monastic teachers, Abba Moses was once visited by a man who wanted some sound advice from him. Abba Moses told him "Go sit in your cell, and your cell will teach you everything."[1]

1. *Apoth. Moses* 6. In Benedicta Ward, *The Sayings of the Desert Fathers*, 118.

Micah, I have times in ministry when I want to quit. For about a year it was *so* strong. The only thing I kept saying to myself was, "Just one more day. Just one more day." Eventually the days were shorter and I could say, "Just one more week." Now I'm saying to myself, "Just one more year!" Eventually your passion will blind you to clock and calendar and you'll look back on this situation with pride and joy.

14

❧ Time Management

Micah,

Time management is one of the most neglected, yet most crucial, aspects of ministry. It's something that, for whatever reason, fails to receive attention in most of the practical ministries classes you'll take in seminary. Yet most of what you will be able to accomplish in ministry will depend upon your proficiency in managing the time that God has given you. At the risk of giving you unwanted advice, let me share some of these principles with you that will help you to manage your time in a Godly manner.

Plan Your Work

First, *figure out what needs to be done.* This includes two aspects: 1) the things that need to be done on a weekly basis and 2) those projects that are coming up that need attention. It will take some time to figure these things out, but once you do, you'll be better equipped for the second part, *scheduling the things that need to be done.* If you can put everything that needs to be done for the week on a task list or task schedule, I think it will help regulate your work efforts and not let you get bogged down with projects that pile up on you. Start with the time-sensitive projects (meetings, things that have deadlines, etc.) and plan your other work around those things.

Here's how it works for me. Every Saturday morning I set aside one hour to plan out the following week. I spend half an hour looking at my calendar, my list of responsibilities and the list of things that need either to be completed or worked on. I look, not only to the week ahead, but to the month ahead, and sometimes to two months ahead. Once I've got the task list done, then I go back and begin to slot those responsibilities onto a daily calendar. The calendar runs from 8:00 a.m. to 9:00 p.m., for seven days. I keep evenings and Thursdays shaded as a simple reminder to generally stay away from them if possible. The first things I schedule are worship services, classes I'm teaching, staff meetings, lunch appointments, and other meetings I'm conducting. Then I go back and schedule my preparation for those events. If I'm leading a meeting on Saturday morning, I'll spend an hour preparing for that meeting on Friday afternoon. During the off times, I'm working on other responsibilities and things that may be coming up two weeks from now. I think you get the gist of the plan here. Putting everything onto a daily calendar helps me see how what I do *today* affects my performance *tomorrow*. It also keeps me diligent in my work.

Work Your Plan

This all takes diligence and self-discipline. There is no point in making up a task list and a schedule of daily work if you're not going to stick to it. Sure, there will be times when you need to set your plan aside to deal with sensitive issues or people who need your compassion and mercy in the moment. (To account for those emergencies I only schedule about 80% of my day. That leaves room for unplanned interruptions and still keeps me on track. If nothing comes up, I move on to the next item during that time.) Keeping a daily work schedule will help you manage your time and will help you accomplish the things you want to get done in ministry.

I've always been a fan of Steve Mariucci, who used to coach the San Francisco Forty-Niners and later the Detroit Lions. I once heard that he had a clock on the wall behind his desk in his office that had no numbers, but had twelve words: "*Now.*"[1] Mariucci reportedly said that it was a continual reminder to him that if something was important enough to do, it should be done right then. Important things should be done "*Now.*" That used to guide my thinking on time management. In fact, I even sought to have a clock like that made. But that mind-set caused me a great deal of stress over the years, and led me to believe that I could never rest from my work, because it had to be done "*Now.*" I've come to realize the wisdom in this state-

1. Thomas George, "Pro Football."

ment: *"Now" is not the time for everything* (Eccl. 3:1-8). Some things need to be done now and some things need to be done later. Some things don't need to be done at all. More on that another time.

It's a shame that most of my colleagues and acquaintances in ministry don't manage their time any better than they do. I know a few who get up around 8:00 a.m., rush through the morning preparations, get the kids off to school, arrive at the office at 9:00 a.m., go to lunch appointments at 11:30 a.m., leave from there to attend the hospital visitations, back to the office at 3:00 p.m., and back to pick up the kids at 4:30 p.m. They have scheduled little time for personal reflection and meditation, little time for professional development and sermon preparation, and then wonder why their ministries are ineffective. I'd hate to see you wind up in that pattern of work and living. Your ministry is too valuable for that. We have a responsibility from God to "make the most of every opportunity" (Col. 4:5; Eph. 5:16). Work ahead and get things done, so that when the time comes that God needs you available for significant ministry opportunities you can lay your own agenda aside and embrace the present moment.

15

❧ Time Stealers

Micah,

One more counsel about time management. Beware of those things that will steal your time! Time-stealers can get you off track and take up a ton of time that could be better spent on other things if you're not careful. Let me give you a few examples.

I once hand-wrote letters to thirty students regarding a youth conference that we'd be attending the following month, because I thought that the "personal touch" would cause them to respond more favorably to attend the conference. Why couldn't I have typed them, or had a secretary do so? Because I was after the "personal touch." The personal touch is to be commended, mind you, but did I really think that hand-writing all thirty of those letters was more personal than a phone call? What could have been done in twenty minutes took three hours. That time could have been better spent talking to students one-on-one.

Broken technology will steal your time like nobody's business! I remember working on an appendix for my doctoral dissertation, and the computer I was using had a tendency to lock up on me. (It had an operating system that was on the market for a year and then quickly yanked for that very reason.) It would normally lock up four or five times a day. The editing that should have taken two hours to complete took six hours. My whole day was shot, and I had to scramble the next day because the things I had planned to complete didn't get done. I don't know how you solve this problem. We were fortunate enough after that to have a separate computer that I could work on while our IT Team fixed problems at the office.

Every church has that person who loves to come to the office a couple of times a week just to hang out and chat. This is the person who has no problems, no ministry concerns, or issues to discuss. He's just bored on Wednesday afternoon and likes to come and chat with you. Now don't get me wrong here: spending time with people in the congregation is a great idea. You have to do this in order to be respected and to have buy-in for your ministry. The person I'm talking about makes a regular habit of coming to your office and staying for an hour or two. You'll have to figure out a way to deal with this if you don't want your time eaten away to the point where you can't be effective. I once went into the office of a college president, uninvited, just to chat. He stood up, talked to me for a couple of minutes, and then said, "Well, thanks for coming in. It was great to see you, and I hope you stop in again the next time you're in town." He didn't give me a chance to sit down and get comfortable, and ushered me out of his office before I knew what was going on!

For me that person was actually someone on staff. He'd come into my office and sit down while I was working. I'd say, "Hey, what can I do for you?" His response would usually be, "Aw, nothing. I'm just in-between projects and wanted to take a little break." He'd then proceed to engage me in conversation about things only he was interested in. I finally had to say to him, "Look, I like you, and I want to help you if you have a problem. But you and I both have work to do." Don't be rude in dealing with these sorts of situations, and don't communicate to those around you that your time is too valuable to be bothered with mundane things like letters and computers. But do be aware of those things that will steal your time and cause you to be unprepared for the ministry tasks ahead of you. Everybody has them. Deal with them firmly, but graciously.

16

❧ Friendship in Ministry

Micah,

I'm glad to hear that you've made some close friends there in the Oriole Street Church. I sensed your frustration before, that ministry was causing you to become isolated. You mentioned once that you thought that God was teaching you about solitude, but solitude and isolation are not the same thing. We were created to be in community with one another ("it is not good for the man to be alone," Gen 2:18), though we all need times of withdrawal for spiritual renewal and communion with God.

When I attended Meadowbrook University, and then worked in ministry with those who were trained there a generation before me, the sentiment was, "Don't make friends in the churches. It will only complicate things and make it harder when you have to leave." I later found out that many who took this attitude *had* to leave because they weren't willing to invest in the lives of those with whom they were ministering. Many of them seemed to minister *to* the congregation, not *with* them. I decided long ago that I couldn't do ministry that way. One minister strongly counseled me not to make friends from the congregation, and I followed him on that. I later came to discover that he'd been betrayed by his best friends in that church. His irrational response was to never make friends again. At that time I began to wonder how many of my seminary professors who counseled the same had similar experiences.

Jesus didn't do ministry that way (he had the Twelve as his close friends, Peter, James and John even closer), and neither will I. I've made close friends in every ministry situation to date, and I'm better for it. Sure, there is the possibility that someone will attempt to make friendship with you under false pretenses, but my guess is that you'll pick up on that right away. Those who are genuine will serve you as much as you serve them, and they'll support you when ministry gets tough. These are the kinds of people I call "Garden Friends." ("Kindred spirits," Anne Shirley would say!) When Jesus went to the Garden the night before his betrayal, he took Peter, James and John deep into the Garden with him (Mt. 26:37; Mk. 14:33). Ministry was about to get really complicated and painful for him, and he needed his friends there to support him and comfort him. Do your Garden Friends ever fall asleep on you? Absolutely they do. And you'll fall asleep on them. But when you get to the place where you can rely on them for anything at any time and for any price, you'll know you've got a Garden Friend. I had three at the Springfield Church: Chris, Bruce, and Bob. And though I no longer live in that part of the country, I still keep in touch with them, and we still get together every now and then. I know that if I were to call them at any moment, they'd drop whatever they were doing and come to my aid. And I'd do the same for them. I have a couple of Garden Friends here in the Walnut Street Church also.

You can't live or work in isolation. That feeds burnout and offers no cure for the times when you want to quit. I know it's hard to move from college to a local ministry situation. In college your friends are close, and you do a lot of stuff together. Local ministry removes you from them and places you in a whole new scenario where you don't know anybody that well. Keep your chin up, lean on your new friends there, and lean on me anytime you need a friend. Any time, for anything, at any price, call me.

37

17

❧ Staff Relationships

Micah,

Staff relationships are tricky, and your concern is valid. Putting two people together in any relationship can be volatile for all of the factors involved, but now that you'll be adding a third to the mix, the potential for disaster is greater. You're fortunate enough to have an administrator there who makes encouraging you a regular part of his ministry, and who is willing to give you the flexibility in your schedule to deal with sensitive issues related to your family. I gather that he's willing to do so because you've been diligent with your schedule and your work load in the past.

No matter what you feel about the new person coming on board, make it your resolution right now to support the team in all situations. No matter whether you agree with the decisions being made or not, resolve now that you will support those decisions in spite of your disagreement. If you can't, this newfound staff scenario (which I sense from you is tenuous already) may crumble. I had an administrator once who, when questioned by the congregation about something I was doing, made it his standard reply, "Well, I don't know about that. I'll have to talk to him about it." He'd then come to my office relaying the complaint of someone who didn't have the integrity to address me personally, and then questioned the decisions I'd made, automatically and unapologetically defending the person who brought the complaint. He always felt that the congregation was more important than the staff (though as a staff member he failed to recall that I, too, was a member of the congregation). I had another administrator who, by contrast, made it his policy to say in those situations, "I trust that he's made the best decision available to him at the time. If he's chosen to go that route, I'm sure he had an excellent reason for doing so. He usually thinks things through pretty thoroughly, and I trust his decision. If you'd like more information, you'll have to talk to him about it." Now I ask you, in which situation do you think I performed better? Do what you can to make the staff environment a positive one from the outset.

Every time we hire a new staff person (and I've seen them come and go frequently) I go through the same cycle. I begin by keeping my distance for the first three months. New staff are bombarded with people who want their attention right away. I intentionally keep my distance and will step in when the mob has left. I want the staff to know that I'll be there for them when everyone else is gone. After about three months, I develop a good relationship with that staff person. My wife and I will have them over for dinner, get to know one another very well. This is about the time that we begin to serve together in some formal capacity within the church. After they've been here about six months, I begin to notice all the faults and weaknesses. I get discouraged by them and they make me wonder whether this person was right for the job. (Every time I say that I won't get bogged down in this, but I do. It's a hard cycle to break.) Once I've come to terms with their weaknesses, and realize that faults and weaknesses make us all special (they're actually the flip side to our strengths), then I settle into working with this person and we begin to perform together in a comfortable manner. I hate to go through this cycle, but they likely go through the same cycle with me.

Perhaps a time of sharing among the staff about what you expect of *one another* (not just what the administrator expects of everyone else), what you see as the greatest strengths of each staff person, admitting your weaknesses up front, and sharing your passions, would help to overcome the hurdles you have described. Structure moments to spend time together, whether it's eating lunch together once a month, going to a ball game, a staff retreat, or simply watching the playoffs together. You won't learn to work together until you love each other, and one of the best ways to learn to love each other is to spend time together.

18

≈ Don't Talk—Deliver!

Micah,

It was good to hear from you. It sounds like you're starting to get a vision for where this ministry needs to go. I know you've been frustrated so far by not having that vision, but it takes time. Little of lasting value can be done in under six months, and sometimes not even in a year. Solid direction, the kind of direction that lasts for more than the length of any program, and the kind of direction that can alter a church for the greater good of the Kingdom for many years to come, takes time to develop and longer to implement. I know you're anxious to make a dent in the gates of Hell for the glory of God, but you don't storm the gates of the enemy without a battle plan and without allies in the conflict. Battle plans take time.

Let me caution you about something else, though. (Please don't assume that I see this in you at this point. I'm going through something here at Walnut Street that is troubling me and I don't want to see you fall into this trap.) It's one thing to "sell the vision" and create the awareness of the things that need to be done. But make sure that you don't just talk. Deliver!

We just hired a staff member to come and help us in the area of Worship Ministries. He's a fine young man, and he's got a lot of good ideas. But that's all they are—ideas. In the last six months he's addressed the staff on five different projects that he would like to pursue, and challenged us on components of the services that need to be changed. To date, he's not taken one responsibility for implementing those changes. It's not that he doesn't have the authority, or that he's waiting for some other committee to take the preparatory steps. He's simply talking a big talk and not delivering on the promises he's made to this congregation. I need to have this conversation with him later today. I dread it, but it's got to be done.

On the other hand, we've got another staff member who very seldom says much. He doesn't seem to have many good ideas. In the six years that he's been here I've seldom heard him pitch an idea for a new program. It used to bother me, but in the last year I've been watching him carefully and I've come to realize that he won't say a word about it until he's ready to pursue it. When he does, he goes whole hog into that project and succeeds almost every time. He's content to let his actions speak for themselves, and the more I notice him, the more respect I have for his methodology, his work ethic and his contribution to the Kingdom in this place.

So that's my advice to you: don't talk—deliver! Part of the delivery process will be what the self-appointed experts call "selling the vision." Make no mistake about it. You won't get people on board if you don't talk. It's the beginning phase of any project. But people will respect you more if you keep your teeth together and let your hands do the talking.

Again, it's not because I see this in you, but only because I'm dealing with it and I wanted to pass this along.

19

❧ Know Where You're Headed

Micah,

One thing that will help with the major program that you're developing there at the Oriole Street Church is to know where you're headed long-term. The program currently under construction is a fine idea. Now ask yourself this question: "How does this program help us achieve our long-term goals here?" It's one thing to pull students into the weekly program that you have in mind (I think "Underground" is a fabulous idea, by the way), but how does it help you with your long-term goals? Do you have any long-term goals for these students?

Knowing where you're headed long-term is what separates the men from the boys in ministry. I know plenty of ministers and churches who are program-happy, who simply listen to what other people are doing in ministry and who are trying to imitate their success by imitating their programs. (We too often neglect the fact that Paul says, "God made it grow" [1 Cor. 3:6].) You'll have a church which grows to two or three thousand in attendance and the minister will be invited to speak at a number of conferences at which he describes all of the innovative things that they did and the structure they adopted to allow that growth to happen. Frustrated ministers whose churches are not growing become excited about achieving the same growth where they serve and try to implement the same programs without doing the hard, necessary work of setting their own vision and long-term goals that are born from an acute understanding of their own weaknesses and strengths. The programs fail miserably in the smaller scenarios, ministers get more frustrated, and eventually decide to try another program from another large church. (And you could repeat this scenario in areas like Youth Ministries, Worship Ministries, and Children's Ministries.)

It's okay to adopt and adapt programs from other places and tailor them for your own needs. Just make sure that you have a long-term plan for the work you're doing and that every program, every lesson, every retreat and outing that you do propels you one step further toward the achievement of those long-term goals.

Here at Walnut Street we have a set of objectives that we want every member to achieve, a list of core values that we want every member to adopt and a list of core activities that we want every member to participate in on a regular basis. Everything we do, from the worship service to Bible School, to the midweek program to the church picnic can be clearly explained as providing members with opportunities to participate in the core activities that we have set as our long-range desire for every person in the Kingdom in this place. Every time someone suggests, say in a Staff Meeting or an Elders Meeting, that we should try this particular program, the next questions on everyone's lips are, "How does this help us achieve our objectives? What core values does this program touch on? And what core activities does this allow the congregation to participate in?" It's hard work, but it's liberating.

Most ministers don't want to do this because it doesn't bear immediate fruit and the time it takes to develop and implement this kind of long-term direction is deemed better spent on other "ministry" items. What you have to set up in your mind is that this *is* the work of ministry: providing structures and environments in which God can transform the hearts and minds of his people. Paul says, "God made it grow," but he prefaces his statement with, "I planted the seed and Apollos watered it" (1 Cor. 3:6). Planting and watering are not easy tasks. So develop and communicate your long-term objectives for those students and plan your events and programs in such a way that they contribute to the achievement of those plans and goals. Sure, sometimes you won't make it. Sometimes you'll think those programs point in the right direction and when all is said and done, they don't! (We've had that here more than I care to admit to you.) Keep at it and you'll see God do amazing things as a result of your efforts.

20

ॐ Take Care of Yourself

Micah,

It's exciting to hear about your long-range vision, your goals and objectives for ministry, and the success that you're having as a result. I got the sense, though, when I spoke to you last that you're overwhelmed with the newfound success in ministry there at Oriole Street. I could sense in your speech, in your tone and in your demeanor that, while you enjoy the work of ministry (especially the changes you see in students' lives), the pace is getting to you.

Don't neglect the care of yourself in the process. Taking care of yourself is a forgotten discipline in ministry these days. It's not readily taught at the seminary, and everything else you hear from those who pay your salary there at Oriole Street says that they expect you to work long and hard for it. Your responsibility and integrity in ministry (the kind that attempts to demonstrate that ministry is the most noble work by the schedule that you keep) is to be commended. But if you neglect the care of yourself in the process you'll only find yourself on the losing end of a long hospital bill. You'll tend toward ulcers, nervous and mental breakdowns, heart disease brought on by high-stress environments, and depression, not to mention the everyday symptoms of irritability, a weakened immune system, and an overall crankiness that will alienate those who have helped you in the management of this success.

You simply must care for yourself as a vital aspect of your ministry. Your body is a temple of the Holy Spirit (1 Cor. 6:19), and the manner in which you care for your body should befit the attention you would give to the Temple of God were you its only caretaker. It's easy to neglect exercise when you're in a high-stress ministry environment. Believe me, I know! The paradoxical reality is that when you're exercising on a regular basis you're less stressed and better equipped to handle the mental pressures that encroach upon you. And it's easy to neglect proper eating, especially in the work you're doing with students. Once your metabolism changes your eating habits must also. Above all, you need time for rest and recuperation. Ministry, like any job, takes a serious toll on you during the course of any week, and if you don't take the time to set it aside and recuperate, you'll be less effective in the long run.

All of this is intricately involved with time management, and exactly how you structure your schedule for these things will be your decision. Take the freedom to schedule these things according to your body's natural rhythms. I run on a daily basis, but I don't run in the morning. I run best in the afternoon, so I like to get up and come to the office early in the morning, get a running start on the day, and then either run over my lunch hour, or run immediately after I get home for the day. I take one day a week off, and I don't let anyone or anything intrude upon that time. I take my calendar in January and I block off that day every week for the coming year. If anyone wants my attention that day, I simply say, "I'm sorry, I have a prior commitment that day." It's my commitment to my family and to my own well-being. I've been criticized for being too inflexible about it, but most people are graciously accepting when they understand that it's also a commitment to ministry with the Walnut Street Church and to the Lord. If I'm to be at my best six days a week, I need one day of rest and recuperation. That one day makes me a better minister for the other six days. Most people appreciate that and respect it.

So do what it takes to rest, recuperate, and take care of yourself. Don't think of this as a selfish, indulgent act that places the highest value on self and not the service of others. Sacrifice of self for the good of others is indeed the highest love: "Greater love has no one than this, that he lay down his life for his friends" (John 15:13). Rather, see it as necessary preparation for long-term ministry. Your ministry will only last as long as you do!

21

ॐ Spiritual Development

Micah,

In my haste to convince you in my last letter about the importance of taking care of yourself physically, I neglected to encourage you also to attend to the development of your spirituality. Taking care of yourself is a two-sided coin, and both aspects require attention and development. Without one or the other you'll become stagnant in your faith and in your ministry. Without both, you'll be no better off than had you never come into the Kingdom.

Were the average person who attends either of the congregations we serve to read this letter, that person might think, "Well why should two ministers be talking about developing themselves spiritually? Ministers, by nature, are spiritual. Therefore, spirituality is a by-product of who they are." You and I both know that this is not the whole story. Paul would have been considered a "spiritual" person, but by his own admission he was carnal, constantly waging war with the sin that was at work in his mind and his "members" (Rom. 7:18–23). Being a spiritual person comes neither quickly nor easily. If we expect to be effective in leading others into Christ-like spirituality we must become the kinds of people we're asking others to become. The spiritual life is not designed for those in vocational ministry alone. Christian spirituality is the call of every believer. If we don't set the example and lead in the development of our own expression of faith, those we work with will never catch the vision of what the devoted Christian life is all about.

Your spirituality is the spring from which your ministry flows, and the base of authority from which you serve. People endowed with the Spirit of God will only respect you long-term if they see the Spirit of God flowing within you. "Deep calls to deep," the Scripture says (Ps. 42:7), and they'll know if you are spiritually full or spiritually bankrupt. Time was when all you had to do was put on the ornamental ministry robe and people would look to you for leadership. A ministry person a generation ago could dismiss charges of impropriety simply because he held the office. "Well, he'd never do that. He's a priest!" Those days have come and gone. In our generation, people will respect you because they know that the authenticity of your walk with God is unmistakable.

Where do you begin? That's a good question. (I sensed you were about to ask this question as you read this.) I would start by exploring the classic disciplines of Christian spirituality: prayer, Bible study, personal and corporate worship, holy reading, solitude, and simplicity. Each of them is a tool to be used in the cultivation of a heart where the Spirit of God can grow. They're not to be used religiously, as tasks to be accomplished to make God happy. Rather, they are tools to be used when the time is appropriate. (You don't use a hammer for *everything*, only when the job calls for it.) Let me suggest three resources that will help you in your journey into the classic disciplines. Richard Foster, *Celebration of Discipline*[1] (now approaching 30 years in print) is the standard work on the subject. This text is a must-have for every minister. M. Robert Mulholland's *Invitation to a Journey*[2] gives you another perspective on some of the same disciplines. And finally, Marjorie Thompson's *SoulFeast: An Invitation to the Christian Spiritual Life*[3] is a very practical text, but has many elements common to the female psyche built into it. For that purpose, I find it very helpful. It stretches me beyond male spirituality.

There's so much more I want to say about this, but there's much more here than you can now possibly bear. Considerations of the time and effort involved are critical. It takes work, and it takes time. Your quest to develop spiritually, much like a physical development regimen, cannot be a program that you incorporate into your life for a few months and then move on to something else. It must become an integral part of your life. Paul counsels us to "continue to work out your salvation with fear and trembling." That's the effort part. The good news is that he doesn't stop there, but continues to

1. Foster, *Celebration of Discipline*.
2. Mulholland, *Invitation to a Journey*.
3. Thompson, *Soul Feast*.

say, "for it is God who works in you, to will and to act according to his good purpose" (Phil. 2:12–13). Put some effort into your spiritual development, and God will transform you by his grace through those efforts.

22

◈ Integrity

Micah,

There's a lot of talk about integrity these days. Nearly all of the conferences I attend have something to say about integrity, the need for it and the benefit it has for ministry. It used to be that integrity was something we took for granted. We all assumed that the minister of the gospel had integrity. The world is a different place now. American culture struggles to find integrity in the workplace, but ridicules those who demonstrate it in everyday practices.

The Church must be having a problem with it or else it wouldn't be a topic for discussion at all of the ministry conventions. In fact, I *know* that the Church struggles with integrity (or lack of it) in professional ministry. The television evangelists who were discovered to be having affairs a few years ago have brought scandal to the Church and led most people to believe that *every* minister behaves this way. I was informed some years ago by the leader of a major youth ministry convention that, in the city in which they host the convention, sale of pornographic movies in that city's hotels skyrockets during the week of the conference. But it's not just sex stuff. I'm increasingly hearing reports of indiscretion with finances, lying in the pulpit and to the Eldership about job responsibilities, and ministers wasting their time and the church's (and the Lord's) by saying they're one place and then doing something else.

I've struggled to define integrity over the years. Is it just about "doing the right thing?" Partly, but not wholly. The word "integrity" comes from a verbal root that denotes completeness, or wholeness. To have integrity means that you are a whole person, or a complete person, that your standard of righteousness, purity and holiness is not just a public spectacle, but rather saturates everything that you say and do. Having integrity would mean that you are honest, not just about your taxes, but on every report that you fill out, whether it be for the government or for a resume. Having integrity means that you are faithful to your wife, in public and in private. If you have integrity, pocketing money after a youth event will never be an issue.

My father used to say, "Integrity is who you are when no one is looking." I didn't understand what he meant at the time. I thought he was being elusive by describing a difficult concept with a riddle. Now I understand. What you do when no one is looking is a huge component of who you are. In fact, that may be your true self. Strive to make your private self the same as your public self and you'll be known as a person of integrity.

Time will eventually prove the man of integrity, Micah. If you have integrity, you'll never have a career-ending accusation stick. You may be accused, but if your integrity is demonstrated and visible, you won't be ruined because of it. The converse is also true. Time will eventually ruin the man with no integrity. Let your faith, your commitment to the greater good of Christ and his Kingdom, penetrate everything you do and integrity will come naturally to you.

23

❧ Trust

Micah,

So I'm watching *Braveheart* the other night (one of my all-time favorite movies), and I came across an interesting concept. William Wallace has just gone to the meeting of the local landlords to discuss the possibility of war with England. The negotiations have led nowhere. Robert the Bruce comes to Wallace and exhorts him to "give these men courage!" Wallace responds, "Men don't want courage. They want freedom. Give it to them, and they'll follow ya."

I got to thinking about our work with volunteers in our ministries. Certainly one of the large components of your work there is the recruitment of volunteers for ministry. No church can operate without volunteer hands for the effort, and no minister will be successful without pulling others around him to help him in his work.

So often the mistake that many ministers make is micromanaging their volunteers. I see this over and over again—a minister recruits a volunteer for a particular ministry, but won't allow that volunteer to have a say-so in the planning, execution or refinement of that particular ministry. Ministers of this sort recruit the volunteers, tell them what to do, tell them what to say, give them the lesson material, ask them not to deviate from it, and then watch this person become very discouraged and quit. It's then that these types of ministers say, "Well, she wasn't very committed to our vision anyway."

Men and women who volunteer in Christ's army don't want a position or a title. What they want is the freedom to do what God has called them to do, the freedom to make the choices and decisions in the ministry of the Spirit that will enhance this ministry, and to impact the world for the Kingdom. That requires *trust*. If you don't trust the people you're working with, your ministry will be marked by suspicion and policy management. (Policies are generally made to quell the fears of policy-makers that employees and volunteers will not say or do things that will embarrass the policy-makers.)

If you can't trust the people that you're working with, don't recruit them. Those who give of their time and energy for Christ and His Kingdom deserve the dignity of partnership with the Spirit of God in the congregation they call home. Just because we have degrees in professional ministry doesn't mean that we're better equipped for every ministry than the entire congregation. It *does* mean that we've been given the tools to train them to be efficient in their own ministries, and if we don't give them the freedom to do what the Spirit of God is calling them to do then we're impeding His work.

Do volunteers need to be trained? Absolutely. Do they need to work together to achieve synergy around common goals? Absolutely. Will there sometimes be disagreements in which you'll have to make a decision that will not be popular with your volunteers? Absolutely. Do you simply hand over stuff to a volunteer and give them no direction for their ministry? Absolutely not. I'm not saying that you give them no direction. What I *am* saying is that we should trust the people that we're working with, and if we can't trust them, perhaps it's time that we end our relationship.

24

❧ Accountability

Micah,

There's a flip side to this "trust" thing. I stand by what I said in my previous statement: you have to trust the people you work with. But I need to qualify that by saying that you must also have account-ability with the people you're working with. Trust and accountability go hand in hand. You can't have one without the other. I only trust you because you have proven yourself accountable with my trust in the past. You're the kind of person who shows up on time to appoint-ments, who does the right thing even when it hurts, and all of this is visible to your peers (hence the accountability). Therefore, I know that if we were working together and I handed off a project to you, that it would be done well.

The kind of accountability to which I refer is tempered with the kind of patience and kindness befitting of the Spirit of God. There is a brand of accountability that smacks of control and fear. It's the kind of accountability that has those in control looking over my shoulder to point out every flaw that I make in ministry. It's the kind of accountability that instills fear in its employees and volun-teers for not doing what is expected. It's the "Big Brother" mentality. (If you've read Orwell's *1984* you'll know what I'm talking about.) This brand keeps everybody in line and doesn't allow them to color outside the lines.

The kind of accountability that is noble can best be illustrated this way. Ever see the movie *First Knight*? Sean Connery plays King Arthur, and he's with his knights at the Round Table in Camelot. Malagant, the rogue knight, bursts into the chamber and accuses Arthur of being a tyrant. He accuses Arthur of making laws for Camelot that only serve to subjugate the people as slaves to Arthur's tyranny. Arthur responds with a fabulous definition of accountability: "There are laws which enslave men and laws which set them free."

Micah, you must have "laws" for your volunteers. That's the accountability part. But make sure that they're the kinds of laws which set them free for ministry. That's the trust part. For example, I counsel the staff here at Walnut Street about their work habits in this manner. We don't say, "You are expected to be here at 8:00 a.m. and work until 5:00 p.m." You have a similar situation there at Oriole Street in that there are many ministry events that take place in the evenings when the volunteers are available. To say, "You have to be here from this time to that time" sets a limitation on our staff that is unrealistic. Do we have guidelines for the work habits of our staff? Yes. In this particular area our guidelines say, "Every staff person is to demonstrate a work ethic that earns the respect of the members of this congregation and its community." That's a law that sets our staff free to do their ministries well. Every staff person is asked to report on their work habits, but our administrators are instructed, if there are questions, not to accuse them of laziness or imply guilt until they've found out all the facts. They are to be trusted in the midst of this accountability. (Of course, it helps that we only hire people that have proven their trust in the past. Hence, we have few problems in this area.)

I don't know what the perfect balance is for you and your ministry there, with staff or volunteers. Volunteers need to have the freedom to do what God needs them to do. They also need to be accountable for the direction of their ministries and to accomplish the goals set for them. We're all working together in this Kingdom, and we need one another in love and mutual accountability.

25

ð Handling Money

Micah,

I can appreciate your dilemma. You won't want to run them off, but you have to set high standards for your youth workers. Otherwise the students won't respect the ministry and the goals that your sponsors are working so hard toward. Be kind and gentle, but stick to your standards.

On the money issue, my recommendation is always that you spend the church's money as if it was your own. There are two different ways of thinking about this. The first says, "The church budget exists so that we can do things that we wouldn't normally do with our own personal finances." This mentality says, "We can go to conferences, ski resorts, camp, and the amusement park and have a great time together. Not everyone would be able to go if we didn't finance this with the church budget. Spend it up!" The second mind set says, "These people work hard for their money, and they're giving it generously for the work of ministry. I had better be as diligent and frugal with their money as I am with my own." You can tell from my tone which of the two I embrace.

Two things you have to keep in mind here. First, I know that once the money is given, it doesn't belong to the people anymore. Fred can't say to me, "You're wasting my money!" It's been formally given to the congregation for distribution as the Elders—and to some extent the staff—see fit. It's not Fred's money anymore. If Fred's attitude was that the money still belonged to him, I'd have a serious heart-to-heart with Fred about his motives in giving. The responsibility still lies with us to be diligent with the money that Fred gives. It may not be Fred's money any longer, but it's God's money, and He deserves more accountability with His money than Fred.

The second factor lies at the heart of the notion, "We wouldn't all get to participate if we didn't spend all this money." That may be true. You may have some students who don't get to participate in every single thing that you guys do in the course of a year or even a summer. (And man, do you guys do a lot of stuff!) I don't consider that a problem. Sure, some students may have to choose which events they attend. They may be required by their finances to attend this event and bow out for the next one. Those students will be better off later in life, and here's why. Life is about making choices—hard ones—and the fact that they are required, by their circumstances, to make these choices now only gives them advance preparation for life. They'll be more mature in the long run than some of those who attend everything you offer.

Here at Walnut Street we have a hybrid system of this. We ask all of our students to pay for all events not directly related to spiritual growth. Those events that are directly related to spiritual growth, we subsidize about thirty percent. If any student who wants to attend a conference or retreat (i.e., "directly related to spiritual growth") can't go because of money, if they request it, we'll pay the whole thing. We won't pay for a trip to the amusement park or the ski resort (i.e., "not directly related to spiritual growth"). But we do make those funds available for spiritual growth events to students who legitimately can't afford to go.

In all things, even in the midst of those events, spend the church's money like it was your own. If you wouldn't eat at a fancy restaurant on your own money, don't do so when the church is buying. If you wouldn't stay at the fancy hotel on your own budget, don't ask the church to pay for it. If you shop diligently for cheap air fare when you're paying the bill, do so for the church, and don't fly first-class. In the long-run, the people who contribute their hard-earned money to the work of the Kingdom there will respect you immensely if they know that you're handling their money with integrity and responsibility. They'll also be willing to give more if they know you'll handle it well. They're on the giving end of Jesus' counsel, "Whoever can be trusted with very little can also be trusted with much, and whoever is dishonest with very little will also be dishonest with much" (Luke 16:10). If they know you're faithful with their finances, they'll be willing to entrust you with more.

26

❧ Having Children

Micah,

Congratulations! I am so excited for you. Your life is about to become entirely different, my friend. The ultrasounds, watching the baby grow, feeling it kick your hand when you touch her belly, the joy the two of you will share, not to mention the midnight cravings, the wild mood swings and the fact (not opinion to her) that at most points during this pregnancy everything that ever went wrong with the universe can be traced back to your influence—what an exciting time!

I remember when we first became pregnant. We were ecstatic. We had twins during our first pregnancy, so all that stuff I shared with you doubled. I had a wise friend who told me this, and I wanted to pass it on to you. He said, "God is about to teach you some amazing things through this pregnancy and your children that you could have never learned without them. You'll learn so much about the nature and the character of God through this. But you have to look for it." Boy, was he right. I remember the thrill and exhilaration that I felt to create new life. I thought, "Is this what God feels when new Christians are born into His Kingdom?" I remembered lying awake one night, frightened that I might wake up and find that my children had stopped breathing. (You'll go through that too. It's normal. Every parent has that fear.) I remember thinking what it would be like to go through the entire pregnancy, only to have the child die within the first six months. It happened to my cousin. I thought to myself, "How many new Christians born into the Kingdom don't make it past six months? It must feel like the death of a newborn child to the Father."

The thing that got me the most was illness. The twins were about six months old. The youngest was teething and screaming her pretty, little head off. With twins, it's difficult early on, for when one of them wants Mama's full attention, there's still another one to care for. The youngest was clingy for two and a half days and wouldn't eat. All she wanted to do was to lay on my wife's chest as she lay on the couch. After three days, we'd had about all we could take. We really got scared at that point. We knew she was teething, but we also knew that teething wasn't supposed to cause this kind of severe reaction. We took her to the doctor and found out that she was cutting two teeth, had ear infections in both ears, and had a virus that caused blisters in her mouth (what they called "thrush"). It took quite some time to get to the doctor, return from the doctor, have the prescriptions filled and for the medicine to take effect. I remember during that time cradling my youngest child in my arms, taking her to the bedroom, kneeling down beside the bed and crying out to God, "If I could take this pain from her ten times over, I will. No more pain for her."

Micah, that day I learned a valuable lesson about the sacrifice of Christ. I finally understood that God would rather take the pain of suffering the punishment for my sins upon Himself than to see me suffer one minute in the torment of Hell. He would rather suffer himself than to see me in pain. That's the kind of God He is—compassionate and full of grace and kindness. He is not distant from me, but hurts when I hurt and feels pain when I feel pain. I would not have learned that lesson in such a profound way had we not had children. The experience of childbirth and parenting taught me (and continues to) about the nature and character of God.

Enjoy this time. Care for your wife. You have no idea what she's going through, physically, emotionally, mentally, spiritually. I don't either, but somebody's got to tell you about these things, and it's better it come from me than from your wife. And if you value your life, don't tell her that you understand what she's going through. It's the Pregnancy Paradox: your wife wants you to understand her pain, but will threaten your life if you assume that you do!

27

❧ Taking Care of Your Wife and Family

Micah,

Congratulations on the birth of your baby boy! I know that's what you were hoping for, and I'm happy that the Lord has blessed you in this way. You'll have a full-time fishing partner, a golf buddy, and (once he's old enough) someone to mow the yard for you!

I don't know if you've given it much thought at this point, but one thing that I think deserves some serious thought is how you care for your wife and family in the midst of your busy schedule. The reason I say that it deserves some thought now is that I went through some pretty drastic situations at the Springfield church when my children were born. Everybody wanted a piece of my time in ministry, and my family needed huge chunks of my attention early on. My reaction to the whole thing was not temperate, but extreme, and I alienated many who could have helped me in ministry later on by setting rigid limitations on the activities and schedule of both my family and my ministry. I don't want to see that happen to you.

Here's where I am now. I currently allow only three nights per week for ministry stuff. I do my best to stick to that. There are some weeks that the family understands I'll be gone more, but they expect (and I deliver) that it will be made up in the weeks that follow. Any more than three nights a week and I begin to get tired and I have trouble keeping my composure in stressful situations. I know that if I push myself beyond my limits, it will be detrimental to both family and to ministry.

I also do my best to be home at a reasonable hour. I normally come home between 5:00 and 6:00 p.m. everyday and help my wife with the children and dinner. I've been at the office all day where it's generally quiet, and I get to have lunch appointments with people at the local restaurants. My wife has been cooped up in the house all day and is hungry for some release by the early evening. So, I make it a point to come home and take the children off her hands and help her get dinner ready. That means that, if I'm to put in a hard day's work, that I need to be at the office early, and I try to make good on that. Most ministers I know don't come to the office until 9:00 a.m. I try to be there between 7:30 and 8:00 a.m. (sometimes earlier, on few occasions later) so that I can get a good start on the day's work. I need everything off my plate when I go home in the evening or I get restless thinking about it. Being there early helps me get it done and be stress-free when I'm at home.

Your wife will need adult conversation. After being home with the kids all day, she'll cry out for your attention. Give it to her. Structure time in your day just to sit and talk with her. Your marriage will benefit and your life will be much happier. The old adage is true. If Mama ain't happy, ain't nobody happy.

Your children will also need your attention. Make sure that you spend time with them individually (if you have more than one). I try to spend at least 15 minutes individually with each of my four children every day. My children need to know that I care about them as persons, not just as one of a group of children that belong to me. I know that doesn't sound like much, but we also spend time together as a family. We always eat dinner together at the dinner table, not in front of the TV, at 6:30 p.m.

Make sure that you take your allotted vacation time. This can help with your personal stress, but it will also help with your family issues. Your wife and children deserve time when they can expect that your full attention will be given to them without the possibility of phone calls or e-mail.

Well, I'm rambling on about things that you need to work out on your own. I don't mean to come off pushy here. I care about you and your family, and I'm passionate about you *not* making the same mistakes I've made over the years.

28

❧ Vacation Days and Time Off

Micah,

Don't do it. I know what you're thinking: "I'm not sure that I'll be ready by the Fall program, and if I don't stay home and get this work done, I might not make it." I've been there, and I'll tell you this (and I think you need to trust me on this one): chucking your vacation time to stay home and work will only set you further behind. If you don't get out of there and collect yourself, get your head together, and spend time with your family, you'll only pay for it in the long run.

Besides, staying home to work when you *really* need to get away will not get you any more work done. In fact, just the opposite will happen. You're tired. I can sense that in your correspondence and from the phone conversations. You haven't had any time off in almost a year, and if you stay home to work during your planned vacation, you'll be too tired to do much of anything, let alone the right thing. You'd be better off going away like you planned, resting yourself, getting your mind off what is happening here, and then coming back at it strong once you return. I think you'll find yourself more energized to get the work done after a long break, and you'll accomplish more in that one week (rejuvenated) than you would in two weeks without the break.

The same goes for your day off as well. Don't forsake that. You need time away to get your mind off things, to sort out all the stuff that is going on in your head about your work, and to do the things that set your mind, body, and spirit at ease for the week ahead. I normally take Thursdays off, and I make it a point not to come to the office on those days. That was very hard early in my career. For my first fifteen years in ministry, I always lived next door to the church.

It was difficult not to walk over and check the e-mail, or think about work when the building is always in sight. Of course, you also have the faithful few who think that because you live next door that you have no right to any personal time away from the job. (That's a long discussion, and one I'm too passionate about to have in public.) I take that day off no matter what. That's the day I mow the yard, we go shopping for groceries, we read a lot, spend time praying together, and I fish. No work on that day. Sure, sometimes I switch that day to Friday, but usually in situations in which we're traveling for the weekend. In any case, I take that day off and very rarely do I let anything interfere with it.

I'm also diligent with my vacation time. Different people enjoy being compensated in different ways. Some guys like to be away for speaking engagements. Others like to receive cash bonuses. Given the choice, I'd have more time off. I don't care about more money. What I do care about is spending time with my wife and kids, spending time alone on the lake fishing (where I sort out all my internal stuff), and unplugging from the work machine. I work *very* hard while I'm at the office, but that intensity needs release, and I make sure I take every vacation day that I have every year. I find that some of my best ideas for ministry come to me while I'm on vacation. I write them down (so that I don't dwell on them) and flesh them out later. The point is this: freeing your mind from the daily grind can rejuvenate new possibilities for your work.

It's a biblical paradigm. If you have an inkling to do so, have a look at the final week of Jesus' life. I believe that if you count the days correctly, you'll find that on Wednesday of the Final Week there is not one recorded event of Jesus' activity. Nothing he did on that day was worthy of mention in the Scriptures. Luke mentions nothing in his detailed historical research, and the other three who were with him that week don't mention anything either. My best guess is that he was preparing himself for the events to come (probably in the Mount of Olives; Luke mentions that he was spending a lot of time there during Final week; cf. 21:37). I couldn't cite it for you directly, but Martin Luther purportedly remarked that he could get more work done in six days than he could in seven. Taking that time off is important and your ministry will be the better for it. So will you.

29

❧ Sexual Responsibility and Ethics

Micah,

Your question is a touchy one, but worthy of comment. I think you're on the right track here, but since you asked for my opinions, I'll certainly provide them.

I don't recommend you be alone with a female in any situation whatsoever. Period. I don't care what the reason is, and I don't care what the circumstances. There is absolutely no reason for you to be anywhere alone with a female for an extended period of time.

Now let me clarify that by reminding you what I'm *not* saying. I'm not saying that you shouldn't be able to counsel females (teens or adults) who come to your office for help. But when they do, the door should be open (if there's no window in it). If you're at camp counseling a student about matters of faith, make sure others know where you are and that you're visible at all times. If a student happens to drop by your home when your wife or kids aren't around, don't invite her inside. If you're in the church building late at night and someone drops by, turn on all the lights. This is common-sense stuff, and I think you understand this. I know too many ministers whose careers have been ruined simply because they didn't think these issues through.

Now let me give you some scenarios for which forethought is crucial. Don't ever be in a car with a female student alone. Sometimes you'll get the occasional student who will ask for a ride home after an event, and your first inclination will be to say, "It's the nice thing to do." Your sensibilities might tell you that you can take her home and return more quickly than you can wait for her parents to show up and retrieve her. That's the worst thing you can do in that situation. When I worked at the East Union Church I had a male student (who's still a good friend) who lived two blocks from my house. He knew that if I was taking students home from an event, he would always be the last one home. I explained to him that I couldn't run the risk of being out with females in the van late at night, and he completely understood. So did his parents. They were all willing to protect my integrity in that regard. (Of course, two other things come to mind: first, that you should *not* be playing taxi-driver for these events anyway and second, that there are just as many issues with male students nowadays as there are with females. Both of those things require their own discussion.)

Here's the point, Micah. None of this code I'm suggesting to you is arbitrary. It comes from Paul's counsel to "avoid every kind of evil" (1 Thess. 5:22), and that we be "innocent about what is evil" (Rom. 16:19). It's not enough to concern yourself in these matters about doing the wrong thing. We must give thought to the *appearance* of the wrong thing. If it looks suspicious, don't do it. Bend over backwards to avoid that appearance and you'll never regret it.

Should some situation happen, through no fault of your own, that places you alone with someone in a compromising situation, dismiss yourself as quickly and as gracefully as you can and then call someone you trust on your leadership team (e.g., an elder, a staff member) and tell them about it immediately. Even if you do nothing more than ask them to mark down the time, the date and the fact that you called to account for your whereabouts.

The rest you can figure out on your own. I know this is more than you asked for, but this is a trouble spot for many ministers, not just youth ministers, and we can't be too scrupulous in this matter.

30

❧ Professional Development

Micah,

Congratulations on the completion of your Masters Degree! That's a major accomplishment and one I know you've worked for diligently. The Kingdom will greatly benefit from the work you've done in this area. I've never seen anything like it. Again, congrats!

Now I get to have some fun: What do you plan to study next week? I know you're saying, "Next week? I just finished this degree! I'm done learning!" To that I would say two things. First, I know you better than that. You won't stop learning and growing as a person, as a minister, or as a servant of God. Second, I would respond by imitating the speech patterns of Jesus. "You have heard it said by men of old that the road to hell is paved with good intentions. But I say to you that the road to *greatness* is paved with *every-day* intentions." (Okay, Jesus didn't say it, but doesn't that sound like something from the Sermon on the Mount?)

The road to greatness is paved with every-day intentions. If you want to be a great piano player, you have to practice every day. If you want to be a marathon junkie, you have to run and eat right every day. If you want to be a great guitar player, you have to practice your scales every single day. The best NBA players practice during the off-season. Whatever it is that you want to be, you have to work hard at it every day if you want to be great at it.

Teaching is my gift, and I want to do it absolutely as best I can. I want to be a great teacher. That means I have to study every day. I block off the first hour of every day for study, and not just in one area. I read widely and voraciously. In the past year I've read books on spiritual development, leadership, spiritual classics, church growth, astrophysics, ancient warfare, parenting, philosophy, atheism, and commentaries on the books of Scripture I was teaching. The week after I finished my doctoral work my reading list was 1,500 pages long. I find that reading widely helps me to communicate to a broader audience and keeps my teaching informed well beyond my own interests. I should also mention that all of this reading I do is distinctly separate from my personal study of Scripture and prayer, which always comes first in the day. I want to be a great teacher and develop the gift that God has given me. I have to work at it every day, and part of the "working at it" is studying as much as I can in preparation. It prevents burn-out and keeps me fed, intellectually and spiritually. The more that I put in, the more there is to draw from when I teach. Therefore, I have to study on a regular basis to keep my teaching fresh.

Whatever it is that you want to be great at deserves daily attention. It won't work to say, "I want to run a marathon next year," and then wait until the week before to start training. You have to prepare for that every day. Think of the long-term goals that you have as a journey to a grand destination. You'll only get to that far-away place by walking one step at a time. You'll never get there by wishing or dreaming about it.

So congratulations, my friend! One segment of your journey has ended. The next has just begun.

31

❧ Wife and Family's Unwritten Expectations

Micah,

Your questions about the involvement of your wife and family in your ministry at Walnut Street are critical. Don't blow them off. You're kidding yourself if you think that your wife and family aren't involved in your ministry. By this I don't mean formally (though that may be the case), but informally. Their interaction with and support of you during the "on" times and during the "off" hours are critical to your well-being and happiness in ministry. Your wife is a lovely, intelligent, and patient woman. She comes from a long line of preachers, and she understands what occupational ministry in the local church is all about.

I sense that your question really has to do with the unwritten expectations that are placed upon your wife and children by local church members (and sometimes by the church leadership, be it staff or eldership). I've known guys whose candidacy was rejected at a particular church because his wife couldn't play the piano. I've known churches who require their ministerial staff and families to be at every church function, in spite of the fact that some of the elders don't hold themselves to the same standards. I have a young man on my staff who left his last ministry post because his wife and children were being fully administrated (bossed around, really) by his staff administrator. James' position was that whenever they wanted to put his wife and children on the payroll, the administrator could tell them to do whatever he wanted. Until then, James' wife and children were *his* responsibility as husband and father. He had a strong case, biblically, but his employers didn't see it that way. I was leery at first, because I'd heard that he had been dismissed quietly from that congregation. Once I found out that this guy was passionate about ministry, loved Jesus, and was willing to put his neck on the line to stick up for his family, I immediately found him to be the kind of person I wanted working here.

My suggestion is that you and your wife sit down and talk about these unwritten expectations, that you agree to some firm and sensible boundaries, and that you stick to them. Once you have this understanding in place, you'll be in a position to explain to people why your wife and children will or will not be involved in particular areas of congregational life. I know you and your wife, and I know your reputation for intensive involvement in the church, so I don't think anyone will be able to accuse you of pulling back altogether. Set the boundaries, and don't let those unwritten expectations run your family over. Be a champion and protector for them.

32

❧ How to Say "No"

Micah,

You can't say "yes" to everything. I know this comes as no big shock
to you, but I think that sometimes we fail to grasp this idea in all
of its fullness. We ministers are under the delusion that every thing
that occurs in the church, that every person's spiritual well-being,
that every non-believer's personal salvation hinges upon our involvement. There is great seriousness in our task, but our tendency is to
elevate that seriousness within ourselves to a greater height than God
intended. People are important, but the way some ministers behave,
you'd think the clergy were the only ones in the congregation who
could perform the functions of ministry and that, while every person
in the Body is important, *we* are the *really* important ones. If we
didn't believe this, we'd not only allow qualified members of the congregation to teach, preach, lead worship, and make crucial decisions
that affect the life of the church, but we'd actually train them to be
good at it.

So get in the habit now of not saying "yes" to everything. Learn
how to say "no." There's an art to it, and it has to be genuine. Let me
explain how *not* to do this, and that will help you understand what
I'm trying to say.

Jill calls you up and says, "Micah, I need a person to run the
Children's Carnival for Family Fest next month. Would you be willing to do this?" Now immediately you're thinking, "I don't want to
do this, it's not what I'm good at, and I absolutely loathe Family Fest
to begin with." Of course, you can't say all that, since Jill's in charge
of the event. You don't want to crush her enthusiasm, and you know
that your attitude about the event is your own problem, not hers.
So, you say, "No, I can't do that. That's not really what I was called

here to do, and I think you should call Jack to help out with that." What you just said to Jill was this: "I am not willing to do anything outside the boundaries of my job description and I won't bend over backwards to help you." The next time you call Jill to help you in some critical area of Youth Ministry, she will likely remember your comments, and refuse to help you (or worse, do so grudgingly).

Instead, do this. Say, "Jill, I'd love to help you. But this is one area in which I'm no good. I'm not saying that to be distant or to get out of work. I'm just being honest with you. I've done this kind of thing before and had little success with it. I do want to help, so let me recommend three people who you could call who I *know* enjoy this kind of thing." Now you've just communicated to Jill that you want to see her succeed, you're not the guy to help her, and that you know three people who can. Instead of having one option (you), she's now got three to choose from. In two days, call Jill and see if she's been able to land one of those people and she'll appreciate your concern.

You can't *do* everything that goes on there at Oriole Street. You can't even *be involved* in everything that goes on there. But you can communicate to Jill and to others like her that you care about what goes on, that you are not gifted to do everything that needs to be done, that she is just as important in the advancement of the kingdom of God as you are, and that you're as willing to help her succeed in her ministry and she is for yours. You both share equal passion and concern to see one another succeed.

33

ॐ Bitterness

Micah,

It's too bad that you're having to go through this. I sense that it may all be a big misunderstanding, but there's also the possibility of some malicious behavior against you. That doesn't mean that it doesn't hurt, that your spirit is not crushed at this moment, and that you won't have some scars over this in the long-run.

I won't pretend to understand what it is you're going through, but I want you to file this away and then get it out in a week or two when you're ready to deal with it. This will sound corny (it did to me the first time), but it's worth considering.

I went through a very difficult time at the Springfield church. It was one of those life-defining experiences, the kind that reveals who you *really* are to you, your family, and everyone who knows you. It's like putting an orange in a vise and cranking up the pressure— the true essence eventually comes out. I won't go into all the sordid details, but I'll tell you the advice I got from the most unlikely of sources. There was a little old lady who lived across the street from us, and her son came and cut the grass for her every week during the summer. He was an elder of one of our sister congregations in the area, and he knew a little about my own situation, from talking to me and getting the weekly scoop from his mother. He and I were standing in the front yard one summer night. I was explaining how I felt about the situation (evidently with a bite in my tongue) and he was listening patiently. As an elder of another congregation, he had to deal with situations like this all the time. I concluded my words of despair, "I don't know what I'm going to do." Quietly and gently, he put his hand on my shoulder and said, "You can get bitter, or you can get better." There were more words, but I don't remember them.

I kept thinking, "What trite advice. It sounds like the cover of the latest book on emotional pain from Christian Press. If he understood my situation even a little bit he wouldn't treat me with such contempt."

But he wasn't. He was being dead-level honest. And he was right on. I was bitter, and he could tell just by talking to me in those few minutes. I had let this particular situation drive me to become something I didn't want to be. I had become everything that I never wanted to be in ministry: a cranky old man with nothing good to say about the church and no solutions to fix the problems. (Just what the Kingdom needs!) I spent the next six months pondering that question, and now I respond differently to difficult situations. I never saw him again. He died of a sudden heart attack shortly after that. Only in eternity will I get to share with him the impact those few words made upon my emotional and spiritual well-being.

Now I want to share them with you. They won't mean much now. In fact, you're probably saying, "How can he share a sappy story with me at a difficult time like this! Why is he treating me with such contempt!" I assure you that I'm not. It's the dead-level truth. When you're ready to deal with it, get this out, spend some extended time in prayer and introspection, and then give me a call.

34

❧ Your Witness in the Community

Micah,

I think that most ministers go through their entire ministry in a location without a thought to how their witness in the community is perceived, let alone how it impacts the Church, either positively or negatively. I've known ministers who left town with huge debts left to be paid on accounts with local merchants. I've known ministers who ran off with the wives of church members, and even one associate minister who, when leaving town, sold his home to a local buyer with the full knowledge that termites had taken up residence in his basement. He didn't tell the buyer, and the buyer trusted him because he was a minister.

These kinds of situations (and they happen more frequently than you know) all reflect, not just upon the integrity and character of the person doing them, but the reputation of the congregation and that of Christ and his kingdom. What does the person living across from the church building, who sees all of this stuff going on, who hears these tales being told at the local market, think of Christ? He thinks that Christ is a swindler, that God has no integrity, and that if you're a Christian you can do whatever you want and expect to be forgiven. None of those things are true. None.

Everything that you do in the community where you live reflects upon the majesty of Christ. Every video you rent at the local video store instructs people on the holiness of Christ's church. (Remember, when you set up your account, they asked your occupation and place of employment.) Every book you check out at the library, every movie you see at the theater, every meal (or drink) you have in public, every restaurant you frequent, every discrepancy you attempt to reconcile at the local bank, and every car you purchase at the local dealer all reflect upon what people in your community think about Jesus.

It's not as simple as saying, "What would Jesus do?" Jesus didn't do these things because he didn't live in this culture. Besides, Jesus was Messiah, and that carries with it a whole set of privileges and grave responsibilities that no other human being in the world can assume. But it is as simple as saying, "How can I make Jesus look good in every thing I do?" Sooner or later, everybody in that small town is going to know who you are, what you do, and who you represent. That town is smaller than you think! Everything you do reflects upon you, your ministry, the Elders, the staff, the congregation and upon the Lord himself. Teach the congregation this and there'll be no stopping the advancement of the Kingdom where you live.

35

ঐ The Mundane of Ministry

Micah,

There certainly are some times in which ministry is mundane. In fact, the idea that ministry is a fast-paced ride of conversion, preaching, teaching, and "winning the world for Jesus" is grossly misinformed. There's a lot of mundane, every-day living kind of stuff that occupies the central place in long-term ministry. Staff meetings, study, articles for the church paper, lesson preparation, sermon research, e-mail, administrative paperwork, setting up chairs and tables, etc.—all of these (and more) may be part of your experience as a minister in a long-term ministry scenario. Sure, there are conversions, exciting times of preaching and teaching. But the bulk of your ministry will be in *preparation* for those things, not in the activities themselves. Machiavelli says in *The Prince* that "A wise prince must imitate these similar modes and never in peaceful times remain lazy, but capitalize on it with industry, in order to be able to use it in adversity, so that, when fortune changes, it might find him prepared to resist her."[1] In shorthand he's saying, "Use the down times to prepare for the stressful times."

We tend to get the grandiose picture from the Gospels, where Jesus is doing something significant at every turn, or from Acts, where we find Peter and Paul involved in exciting conversations that lead to someone accepting Christ. Those things are the most exciting things in the world. But we tend to forget that the text reads more quickly than it actually occurred, and that there are a lot of things *not* said in the text that indicate for us a whole host of other activity that's less than noteworthy. During Final Week, nothing is recorded of Jesus' activity on Wednesday. I don't know what he did that day.

1. Machiavelli, *The Prince*, XIV.

Maybe nothing. It wasn't important enough for any of the gospel writers to mention. Paul uses Antioch as a launching point for his missionary journeys, but if you'll read carefully, you'll notice there are extended times between the journeys when Paul is in recovery and preparation for the next trip. We tend to see him as coming home, giving his reports, and then heading off the next day on another tour. The disciples in Jerusalem sent him to Tarsus for a while before his ministry began (Acts 9:30). When Barnabas first brought Saul to Antioch, they spent a year doing nothing but preaching and teaching (Acts 11:25–26). When he returned from the first journey, he stayed in Antioch "a long time" (Acts 14:28) before he went out again. After the Jerusalem council, Paul stayed in Antioch for a while before deciding to retrace his steps and visit the churches again (Acts 15:30–36).

What's my point? Show up every day, do the work that's assigned to you, and let God worry about how you're supposed to make a difference. Don't approach every task thinking, "How can I make a *huge* impact for God in this?" Approach every task thinking, "Is this what God wants me to do? And how can I do it with excellence?" Care not whether you become famous while doing these things. Let God worry about your influence. Do these things and do them well, and the rest will take care of itself.

36

❧ The First Grief Visit

Micah,

I remember my first "grief" visit well. I was only 18 at the time. I was working at the East Union Church and the minister was gone on vacation. I got a call from someone at the hospital requesting to speak with the minister. When I assured her that he was out of town, she told me that she was calling on behalf of the person whom our minister visited on occasion. This man was dying, and wanted someone from the church to come over and pray for him. Not knowing what to do, I agreed to go and attempt to comfort them in any way possible. I got to the room, prayed for this man, stayed only a short time, and then left. When I got back to the office, there was a message on the answering machine indicating that he had passed away shortly after I left the hospital.

As strange as that experience was for me (I had heard my grandfather speak of instances very similar to this, but had never experienced one myself), what was more disturbing was that this exact same scenario played itself out the *next* summer while our minister was on vacation! Someone whom he was used to seeing was about to pass away, they requested I come pray over him, I did, and that person passed away while I was driving home. Talk about strange events! The next summer I refused to go pray over *anyone* at the hospital while the minister was on vacation.

The real difficulty is knowing what to do when you go *back*, after the loved one has passed away. What do you say? What do you do? How can you help? Sure, there are a number of books out there that can help you with this (Granger Westberg's *Good Grief*[1] is absolutely the best among them), and this gets a lot of traffic in minister's

---

1. Westberg, *Good Grief*.

manuals and books on pastoral ministry. I've found that the theory and intention behind all of those discussions withers at the hospital bedside. I don't care how prepared you are. If you're human, you'll still struggle with what to do, what to say, and whether you should even be there or not. Some like to pray. Others recite scripture. Still others do nothing but hold the hands of those who are grieving.

Each situation is different, and you'll have to allow the Holy Spirit to guide you concerning what is appropriate. I've been in some grief situations in which Scripture reading was wholly appropriate and meant a great deal to the family. I've been at the bedside in other situations where I shared no Scripture or prayer whatsoever, and the family thanked me for it. They appreciated that I didn't try to "work" them by doing the things that I thought should be done simply because it was expected. They appreciated that I just showed up, held their hands, and wept with them. These were my friends, and to be "ministerial" with them at that time would have been offensive. I know that sounds strange, but you'll know it when it happens.

Long to short, I don't know what to tell you about how to approach your next grief visit. Certainly the first one was painful for you. Uncomfortable, at least. If you're half the man I believe you to be, this will never be easy. It will become less stressful the more you do this, but it will never be easy. Pray for the family before you go, ask the Spirit to guide you, and be carefully attentive while you're with them. Don't get in their way. I like to stand over in the corner. It's their loved one who has passed, not yours. If they request that you pray, sing or read Scripture, do so. Don't lie to them or give them false hope. Truth, though difficult, is liberating even in times of trial. Most of all, love them, care for them, and help them, if at all possible, deal with their grief.

37

❧ Watch What You Say

Micah,

Be careful of what you say to those in your congregation. If you're not careful the things that you say can come back to bite you. Even though the Oriole Street church is growing beyond the wildest imaginations of the staff, and even though there are more people attending there than you can possibly keep up with, that doesn't mean that the things you say are unimportant anymore. In fact, just the opposite is true. You've moved from the mid-sized church to a large-sized church, and the relationship that the staff has with the congregation has changed a bit. Where you used to be a friend to the congregation and were able to speak about things you'd like to do, to bounce ideas around with many of the members of the congregation, now the membership is beginning to see you as a spokesperson for the leadership of the institution. The things you say now are representations of what the leadership *plans* to do, not what they're *thinking* about doing. Certainly, you'll have your inner circle, the group of members who are intricately involved in your ministries with whom you can bounce ideas around. But those folks have to know their own leadership role and not promote ideas as concrete plans.

Where this really comes into play is in the networks of relationships that exist within the church that you don't know about any longer because the church is so large. Though our membership is not as large as the one you worship with, an appropriate illustration will suffice. When I was working at the Springfield church, I was interviewing with other congregations. My discontent there was growing, and I was anxious to leave. I interviewed here at Walnut Street with no expectation that anyone at Springfield knew what I was doing. These two congregations are a thousand miles apart from one another. My interview was on Friday. I flew up Thursday night, spent my day off interviewing, and flew back on Friday night. I went to church on Sunday morning there at Springfield, preached the service, and went to the lobby during the concluding song to prepare to meet the people as they left. One older gentleman came out with his wife before everyone else, shook my hand (told me the usual, "Good sermon, preacher") and then leaned over and whispered in my ear, "I hope you get the job at Walnut Street. That church really needs you right now." (This man had only been attending with us for about three months and, at that time, had no vested interest in running me off. His comments were genuine.) My face turned ghostly white! I was dumbfounded. I couldn't get into it with him there, but later found out that he used to attend the Walnut Street church, had just moved to Springfield three months ago, and that his daughters were still very active at Walnut Street. They made the connection and told their parents that I had interviewed with them.

The point is this: because the relationship networks are unknown to you the larger your congregation becomes, the more imperative it is to watch what you say. To say the wrong thing to the right person can set off a cascading discontent. I had a colleague once who complained to a lady involved in the Worship Committee that the eldership wasn't doing its job and that he was very unhappy with their leadership. He later found out she was the daughter of the chairman of the elders. How that escaped him I'll never know. But the elders soon became unhappy with his leadership and had him replaced within two years.

Of course, all of this talk about "talk" has its roots in your personal integrity. Don't say anything to anyone about a third party that you wouldn't say to that third party personally and you'll be fine. The relationship networks are larger and deeper than you can possibly fathom. Don't let them be your undoing.

38

❧ Responsibility as a Youth Minister

Micah,

I just want to commend you for a moment on your personal responsibility. I see you fleshing this out in your ministry to the students there at Oriole Street, and I wanted to laud you for it. Of course, I also spoke with your Senior Minister this morning about another issue, and he sincerely commended me for recommending you for the post there. He appreciates your responsible approach to youth ministry. I know you feel like every time he says, "Let me encourage you to keep doing things in a responsible fashion" that he's trying to build up something in you that's non-existent. But he's not. Let me give you a bit of perspective on where he's coming from.

Ever since the beginning of my own career, Youth Ministry has had a less than credible reputation as a legitimate ministry within the church. Most leadership boards are quick to say that the second position that should be hired is a youth minister, but seldom do they consider that most people in the congregation see it as a second-rate ministry. (I'm not saying that it is, so let me finish.) As a Youth Minister I used to hear things like, "What do you want to do when you grow up?" and "When are you going to get a ministry of your own?" I even had one Senior Minister openly call my ministry "back door evangelism," referring to it as a benefit to winning souls, but something that we don't want to advertise as a visible ministry of this congregation. Most congregants see Youth Ministry as a stepping-stone to "real" ministry (i.e., preaching).

The primary reason that most adults have such a negative view of Youth Ministry is that they've seen too many irresponsible young men (and women) approach their work with far less responsibility than you are presently showing. Many youth ministers view their work as glorified babysitting, a chance to do nothing but goof off with the youth, or an opportunity to get paid for doing very little work. Many young ministers see their work with youth as simply a matter of planning events and outings and do very little work in evangelism, discipleship and leadership development with youth and parents. When you act like one of the youth and approach your work with the mentality of a teenager, parents in the church won't trust you with their children, no matter how old they are. They won't respect or participate in the long-term work you're doing, and the leadership of the congregation will begin to question the manner in which you represent them to the community.

When our present youth minister came here, he followed a young man who was typical of what I'm describing to you: programmatic, little depth, and little responsibility. The previous youth minister was long on ideas but short on detail. He would organize things at the last minute, fill out permission slips in the parking lot as parents were ready to leave the premises, and provided very little structure for the students on a week-long outing. Needless to say, the expectations from parents weren't very high.

The first week-long conference that our students attended under our present youth minister's direction was well-organized and well-thought. He had a deadline for the registration forms, he told the parents exactly when they were leaving, exactly when they would return, and the behavior he expected of the students and sponsors who were attending the conference. He made sure every student had the pertinent medical information on hand and asked parents to provide him with numbers at which they could be reached in case of emergency. He even insisted that every student wear a seat belt at all times on the van. I know that this all sounds routine to you, but our parents weren't used to this. Their normal expectation was so far removed from this kind of responsibility that they were blown away by his professionalism. When asked why he was doing things this way by a few of the students in the Parents' Meeting, he responded with this: "Your parents are entrusting me with your care for the next six days. It's my job to make sure you attend, behave, and return safely. That responsibility comes first, even before what makes you comfortable." He won a ton of respect from the parents that day, and consequently has more adults involved as long-term coaches in our Youth Department than any youth minister we've had before.

It's difficult for many people in our churches to view Youth Ministry as a bona fide ministry when there are so many who are treating it with far less than the respect it deserves. It's a vicious cycle: church hires youth minister, youth minister works with laissez-faire attitude, church sees Youth Ministry as a subordinate ministry requiring little responsibility or administrative savvy, church reasons in the next search committee that since it's a second-class ministry no standards of excellence are required, church hires another youth minister with a laissez faire attitude, and the cycle repeats itself.

So work hard, be responsible, and approach your ministry as if it's the most important thing in the world. I know you get frustrated with your Senior Minister for encouraging your responsibility. Sometimes we do that because we want to encourage those things that we want to see grow in a person that which is lacking. I assure you, he's not doing that. He's encouraging you because your approach to Youth Ministry is unlike anything we're used to seeing in this field.

39

❧ Working with Difficult People

Micah,

There will always be people who cause problems for you, no matter what ministry you serve. Let me share with you two items which were beneficial for me in dealing with difficult people.

1. *Disagreements stem from passion.* I used to think that those who were causing me problems were simply difficult people who enjoyed watching me suffer. I believed that they wanted to see me fail and that my own leadership wasn't good enough in their eyes. Over the years I've come to understand that the disagreements I have with those in my ministry usually stem from the conflict of the passion that we both have for ministry and for the Lord. Think about it. You don't normally have trouble from people who aren't involved. Sure, occasionally you will, and complaints are different than disagreements. The guy who sits on the back row and complains about everything you do is not what I'm talking about here. The disagreements you have about how to proceed in ministry usually arise from people who are just as passionate about ministry as you are. I first picked up on this in Marshall Shelley's book *Well-Intentioned Dragons.*[1] Most people don't argue because they have nothing else to do. They do so because they have a desire and a passion for ministry.

Our Youth Minister and our Worship Minister used to disagree bitterly about the role that the teenagers would have in our worship services on Sunday morning. It got so bad that I had to mediate a session between them. In that session I pointed out that they were both passionate about their ministries, and that the common ground here was worship. The Youth Minister was passionate about our students becoming actively involved in the corporate worship experi-

1. Shelley, *Well-Intentioned Dragons.*

ence here. The Worship Minister was passionate about everyone else being actively involved in the corporate worship experience and not allowing one ministry department to assume the majority role in corporate worship. (Only one third of our services are made up of the teenagers. To have them run eighty percent of our service would not be good representation on our part.) Each thought the other was belligerent and wanted to cause trouble. Once they saw that they were both passionate about teens being involved in worship (their disagreement was about the *level* of involvement, not involvement per se), they were able to speak to one another respectfully about intelligent and sensible options to achieve both goals. In the early days, the solution was a Youth Sunday four times a year. That eventually evolved into a youth-led worship service that meets every week here at Walnut Street.

2. *"Keep your friends close and your enemies closer."* Yes, you recognize that line from *The Godfather*. (If you've never seen it, do so immediately! There are great leadership lessons embedded within.) One of the best things you can do if you have a person causing you difficulty in your ministry roles is to bring them further into areas of responsibility and involvement in your personal ministry. Again, keeping in mind that those who voice their disagreements with you are communicating their passion for ministry, give them an opportunity to share that passion by working closely with you. When ordered about Luke Skywalker's destruction, Darth Vader said to the Emperor, "If he could be turned he would become a most powerful ally." The Emperor agreed.

I once had a young lady continually complain that she didn't like the direction that the sermons were going on Sunday mornings. She was reasonably involved in other areas, but continually complained that, though the sermons themselves were good, the topical directions of the series were inappropriate for the congregation and didn't meet her needs or the needs of the visitors that she was bringing to church with her. So when I'd had enough of her complaints I invited her to participate in the Sermon Planning Team. After only three months of working on this team she has a new appreciation for the difficulties involved with reaching three or four different audiences in the same room each Sunday morning, the work that goes into crafting a sermon, and the prayerful intention that goes into the sermon direction on a yearly basis. In the year prior to joining the team, she had become a lightning rod for those who weren't content with the preaching direction. Just last week I happened to hear her defending our direction to one of her own chronic complainers. She suggested that person also be involved in the Sermon Planning Team.

So if you have a person who's vocally and publicly disagreeing with you about the direction that you're taking, bring them in close. Don't think of them as an enemy, but consider that if you offer them the chance to be more closely involved one of two things will happen: either you'll have a new ally in ministry, or you'll have the right to say, "I offered you a chance to help in this area and you turned me down." Sun Tzu said in *The Art of War*, "Subjugating the enemy's army without fighting is the true pinnacle of excellence."[2] Win over your critics, involve them in your ministry, and keep them close. Your life and your ministry will benefit immensely if you can handle all of the internal issues involved in doing so.

2. Sun Tzu, *The Art of War*, III.

40

❧ Leadership Development

Micah,

Take great care that your ministry is concerned in part (but no small part) with developing leaders. When I say "leaders," I don't mean the staff people who work with you. It's easy to tell your staff that they need to do this or that and that they should become something they presently aren't. The developing of leaders within the congregation is a vital task that every minister should be about and that I see less and less in today's ministry paradigm.

Many churches have the "CEO mentality" of the senior ministry. The lead minister in many churches is often referred to as the "pastor" and operates as the CEO of the institution. He leads, sets the tone, determines the direction, decides who comes and goes on staff, and seldom asks a team of servant-leaders to come alongside him and learn his trade.

Every minister has to be involved, in some part, in all of those things. But in my opinion this mentality has at least three drawbacks. First, it leads to an isolated, "I'm the guy!" mentality. When ministers operate this way, it sends a message to the congregation that he believes himself to be the Chief Shepherd of this congregation, a title that is specifically reserved for the only one in the universe who paid for it (1 Pet. 5:4). Second, it sends a message to the congregation, "I don't need anyone's help." This is downright arrogant and will lead to isolation and decline in volunteerism. Third, it also sends a message that the ministry of the senior pastor is the most important ministry, and that everyone in the congregation ought to fall in line and help him accomplish his own objectives. The congregation then becomes nothing more than a volunteer army to advance the personal and career goals of the lead pastor.

I understand I'm dramatizing just a bit. But this is my point. Leadership development, developing leaders from among the membership of your own congregation, is a vital aspect of your ministry that cannot be neglected. Here are the benefits.

1. *Developing leaders ensures that you're not working alone.* In spite of what you may have been taught, ministry cannot be done effectively apart from the community that Christ has designed into his Body, the Church. Everything I was taught, both in seminary and from my supervisors early in my career, said, "Don't make friends in the church. You'll only get burned." It's just as dangerous to isolate yourself from the relationships that God has intended for us in the church. When you develop leaders, you ensure that you're not working alone. Your leaders will continually surround you and you'll work together for what God has envisioned for this congregation.

2. *Developing leaders ensures that your work continues in your absence.* It's rare that a minister serves with a congregation for longer than fifteen years anymore. Even in the case of a long-term ministry, this question is important: What happens to the congregation and to the work to which God has called you should you be involved in a terrible accident tomorrow and not live through it? Will the work and ministry God has ordained for you continue in your absence? The only way to ensure that it does is to train leaders from among the congregation to carry on your work—to listen to the Lord as you do and minister to one another. If you develop leaders your work will never cease to reap a harvest.

3. *Developing leaders builds the Body, not just the organization.* Many of my colleagues are concerned with the growth of the organization. (I'm intentionally not using the word "church" at this point.) Their measure of success is the size of the building, the meeting of the budget, and the large numbers of people who come and listen to them on Sunday mornings. I realized long ago that my ministry would be more effective if I trained leaders from among the membership to teach, preach, lead worship and run meetings rather than doing all of those things myself. Sure, it's more difficult to train somebody to do this than it is to do it myself. But in the end, we'll have a Church, not just an organization.

4. *Developing leaders is best done by example.* If you want your leaders to understand the importance of personal Bible study and

prayer, you had better be involved in those things. If you want to train your leaders to teach, continue to teach before the congregation on a regular basis. If you want your leaders to learn how to preach, let them in on your sermon-planning process, hand them the outlines, and ask them to watch you and evaluate as you preach. Don't go to the extreme of recruiting leaders to do *everything* for you. You'll still need to be an active part of those tasks, but now they take on a whole different character. You'll still preach on Sunday mornings, but you'll be asking two or three men to learn from you so that *they* can in turn preach some Sunday morning while you're absent.

Developing leaders is a must for your ministry. Think long-term, and think about the future direction of this congregation, even if you're not there. If things fall apart after I'm gone, many will say that I'm truly missed. If things don't fall apart after I'm gone, but continue to run well without me, some will say that I wasn't needed in the first place. I say that if I leave this place and nobody misses me, I'll have done my job, and done it well.

41

❧ Getting Things Done

Micah,

You're absolutely right. Recruiting, developing and entrusting leaders with great responsibility takes work, but in the long run, you'll accomplish so much more in ministry. Your ministry will have a lasting and exponential success.

Here's another thing to consider. You'll be amazed at what you can get done if you don't care who gets the credit. My grandfather told me this when I first entered the ministry, and I've never forgotten it. I try my best to live by it. If you honestly don't care who receives the praise for the work, you'll be so much more effective. Often we want to do the baptism because we've done the evangelism, we've done the counseling, and we want to have a hand in the actual event. At least that's what we tell ourselves. In actuality, there's a part of us that wants everyone in the congregation to *see* that we've had a hand in this. If I can set aside my pride, and if I don't care who gets noticed for the things I do, I'll elevate those around me and raise the level of awareness and success of the congregation, not my own ego.

So when you've planned a retreat and parents come to you and thank you for putting on a fantastic event, simply say, "Thank you," and remind them that there were other adults who had a hand in making the event happen. If those adults worked harder than you did, point that out. When you've helped someone get their ideas for ministry off the ground and seen them actualized in ministry, remind people that it wasn't your idea to begin with. And when you've planted your own ideas into the minds of your leaders, and they run away with them and make them successful, and when you see that leader being encouraged by others in the Kingdom, do everything in your power to resist the urge to point out that it was your idea in the first place.

If you don't care who gets the credit, your ministry will be so much more effective. It has a humbling effect, and a very successful one at that.

42

❧ Pride

Micah,

The reason for my comments about not caring who gets the credit in your ministry is that pride is the deadly enemy of ministry. If you let you pride run rampant, unchecked, it will destroy your credibility and the Lord's work in your life and in your ministry.

I was having lunch with our Minister to College Students just last week. He seems to be very upset that some of the students who would normally attend his class are now attending the Young Adult class (taught by another staff member here). Evidently, the Young Adult teacher had done some recruitment throughout the congregation, advertising his class in the young adult age group, and some of the college students decided they would participate. The Minister to College Students was very upset because, "He stole my students from me. They should be in my class, not his."

He was a bit disappointed with my counsel. He wanted my advice on how to approach this other staff member and demand that he hand over the students. He wanted these students to return to his class. My line of questioning with him fell along these lines: "Why are you upset? Why do you want them back in your class? Do you feel like they aren't going to learn anything in the Young Adult Class? Do you think your fellow staff-member stole them from you intentionally?" Pride was at the heart of his problem. Deep down he felt like he could teach these students better than anyone, that his class was a better environment for them, and that, while they would grow in the Young Adult Class, his own efforts with them would be much more effective. Once he faced himself honestly and came to the realization that his own pride was a problem, he was able to relax about this situation.

There is a false humility. Don't make the mistake of falling into that trap either. There is a kind of humility that takes pride in being humble. In the end, it's still arrogant and prideful. You'll have to learn to evaluate your own ministries and learn how to receive compliments in a gracious and humble fashion. One of the hardest things to do is to simply say, "Thank you," and nothing more. If you can learn to be genuinely humble and resist the urge to believe that every good thing in ministry revolves around your own efforts, you'll be a well-adjusted person with a healthy view of the Kingdom.

43

ᘒ Recruitment

Micah,

I understand your dilemma. I am *horrible* at recruitment. Well, I used to be horrible at it, and I still don't think I do it very well. Others around the office here disagree. I'm not a salesman. I don't like receiving high-pressure sales pitches, and I don't like to give them. For me, if you have a passion to do it, and the Lord is leading you toward it, a lot of pressure from me isn't necessary. If you have a desire and a passion to serve in that area, you don't need the benefit of a high-pressure pitch. If you're *not* interested, a high-pressure pitch simply pushes you into an area you didn't want to go in the first place, and chances are you won't be inclined to go above and beyond the call of duty if you don't care about what you're doing. I find the high-pressure pitch detrimental and contrary to ministry.

I also used to have problems when people turned me down for various ministry opportunities. I still do to some degree, but not like before. I used to perceive that what I was asking of a particular volunteer was the opportunity to give of their time for the most important thing in the world, the advancement of the Kingdom of God in the midst of any particular ministry department I was working in (at the time, youth ministry). When people would turn me down, I'd think, "How in the world can you say that you have something better to do than to share the life of Christ with these teens? I can't believe how shallow you are!" The profound fear of rejection prevented me from doing recruitment appropriately and adequately. Two things I've learned since then: 1) while the Kingdom is important, I had an over-inflated sense of what I was calling people to do and 2) sometimes people legitimately have better things to do—even God-ordained things—than what I ask of them.

The fact of the matter is that in ministry, if you can't recruit volunteers for the task, you're doomed. You'll either get absolutely nothing accomplished in ministry or you'll burn out trying to do everything yourself. I was in serious danger of falling into the latter category.

Once I recognized my weakness, I was able to pull some people around me who could help me in that particular area. Knowing that I was horrible at recruitment, I "recruited" with great care and intention four people who were great at motivating and encouraging people to serve. They were, in fact, fantastic at recruitment. I was primarily responsible for four different areas of ministry at that time, and I asked them each to serve as a Department Coordinator for one of the four sectors. Whenever we designed new programs, they knew how our strengths were to complement each others' weaknesses. I designed the program (my strength, their weakness) and they recruited the people necessary to implement and execute the program (their strength, my weakness). We were, together, a living example of Paul's illustration of the complementariness of the Body (Rom. 12:3–8; 1 Cor. 12:20–26).

So while I understand your frustration in your inability to recruit volunteers for the Kingdom's ministries, I also have to remind you that there's no "out" here. You simply must find a way to become proficient at this, either through your own efforts or of those around you. Keep wrestling with it. The confusion, the dissonance, the pain you're having over this particular issue is the place of spiritual development. It's where God does his best work. I'm confident that, with time and attention to your own weaknesses and problems, you'll be better for it in the end. So will the congregation and the Kingdom at large.

44

ᴣ♦ Worship Styles

Micah,

I understand your concern about the worship styles. We also face that in our congregation. Several years ago we decided to adopt two separate styles, each meeting in a different room in the building at a different time. Our contemporary service now meets in the Multi-Purpose Room at 9:30 a.m., and our traditional service meets in the Auditorium at 10:45 a.m. Many of our colleagues in ministry said this wouldn't work, that we'd divide the congregation by having two separate styles. But it hasn't happened. We knew ahead of time that we'd have to spend a lot of time talking about unity and diversity. We still focus on that quite a bit. We've come to realize, with Stephen Covey, that "Sameness is not oneness; uniformity is not unity. Unity, or oneness, is complementariness, not sameness."[1]

So why is it that people get upset about the differences and changes in worship styles these days? I don't exactly know. We've stopped talking about "worship styles" and gone to intentionally using the language of "music styles." Worship is never defined in the Scriptures in terms of style. It's defined in terms of obedience, wonder and awe, and doing what God asks of us in everyday living and in group ceremonies. It's a small thing, I know, but it's something that we're doing in an intentional effort to remind people that we're not talking about "true worship" versus "false worship." What we're really talking about is musical style. The other elements of our worship services remain the same from service to service. It's just the music that's different.

Secondly, I think that people get perturbed by other worship styles as a matter of conditioning. I grew up in a very conservative

1. Covey, *Seven Habits*, 274.

church. Hymns were the norm, piano and organ the staple of my worship diet. The day the guy from the local seminary traveling team set up his drum set on stage was a hard day for many people. Why? Because we'd been conditioned that "true worship of God involves hymns, organs and pianos." Had we been taught that intentionally? Never. But we had all worshiped together for many years with that style, and we'd all assumed, by default, that if there was a better way we'd be doing it. We'd never considered another style. Other styles meant the equivalent of worshiping other gods. It was hard for us to get over that hurdle. Now that I'm older, I understand the value of both contemporary and traditional music. I also understand that neither would be recognized in the first or second centuries as a legitimate style. Times change, styles change, and the Spirit of God has given us the freedom to do what makes sense in our own cultural context.

So how do you get past the hurdle? Well, first, the hurdle doesn't just exist for those in traditional worship. Don't make the common mistake of thinking that they are the ones who have to change, grow up, and accept the contemporary forms. That's as arrogant and demeaning as saying that traditional music is the only true style. Everybody has to be mature in these situations, and maturity in Christ has nothing to do with elevating one style over another. It has *everything* to do with your response to the situation. If I don't like traditional music, but I recognize that many will benefit by going to a more traditional approach, if I can walk into that service and truly *worship*, then I've reached a level of maturity that many in our churches today lack. By the same token, if I don't like contemporary worship, but my response is one of gracious acceptance and a willingness to worship God, no matter what the style, then I've reached a level of maturity that is not common. It has little to do with the particular music style and everything to do with my response.

Are there issues with the theology of the contemporary songs? Absolutely, and you have to make sure the songs you sing teach accurate Biblical concepts. But the same applies for the hymns, some of which we'd be appalled by if we really examined their theology. Do we have to make sure that contemporary forms are done with dignity and respect? Absolutely, but no more than we have to ensure that traditional forms are filled with the passionate worship of God and not left to rigidity and inflexibility.

Keep struggling with these things. Model maturity for your membership. Show them that you can attend *either* service and truly worship, irrespective of the style. Model flexibility. Don't exalt one style over the other. Teach the same at all services so that no jealousy exists about who's being fed better from the pulpit. Communicate that everyone is important to the Body, and that our disagreements and differing opinions actually make us stronger.

45

❧ Discernment (How to Make Decisions)

Micah,

Your question about your friend's decision to return as a member to the church that he previously served is an interesting one. I was trained in ministry that you don't ever go back to the place you've ministered and left. I don't always hold to that. Neither did Paul for that matter. He exercised a great amount of influence over churches he'd left. But in this case I think it's wise for Todd not to be there. He's been gone less than six months and I think you're right to note that it could cause conflict. I don't know all of the details of their conversation, or what reasons he gave for leaving, or if he left because he couldn't apply for Brent's job, but I think Gary is correct here. You don't want on staff the kind of person whose demonstrated track record is to make hasty decisions and to leave at a moment's notice.

The larger issue for Todd is how he's making his decisions. I'm increasingly hearing people say, "God is leading me in this direction. God is telling me to do this or that. This is God's will for my life." I sense your question in the first e-mail is how to tell whether Todd is being obedient to God's direction for his life by returning to North Dakota and leaving this other congregation. What he's doing may, in fact, *not* be the will of God. Knowing the will of God in specific, daily situations is something that I've struggled long and hard with in my own life and ministry, and I think I can help you by laying out for you my discernment process. Our Youth Minister just told me today that this process has helped him greatly in his own life, and was the most valuable tool he'd ever picked up in his spiritual development. For me, God's will in life, ministry, and the pursuit of happiness is confirmed in a four-fold process.

1. *Inner Promptings by the Spirit.* The Spirit of God prompts us in certain ways. We all feel this. Unfortunately, many people stop here. Many get an inner prompting and decide, "This is what God wants me to do." The problem is that at any given moment I can be prompted by other things: the un-holy spirit, my subconscious fears and desires, the expectations of others, or the spirit of my wife's meatloaf (i.e., physiological factors—don't make decisions when you feel bad). Most people stop here and that's problematic. These promptings have to be confirmed by

2. *Clear Counsel from Scripture.* Obviously if it doesn't match with Scripture, it's not from God. There are many things that fall into this category, and I won't belabor them here. I don't know if Todd has a situation in which obeying passages from Scripture is an important thing to consider. Many situations in my own life do not. I'm not deciding whether or not to have an affair on my wife. Scripture makes that decision clear. Does it help me decide whether or not to leave Walnut Street and take a teaching job? Maybe. Maybe not. These things have to be confirmed by

3. *Circumstances.* If God is truly leading me to go somewhere else, he'll make the opportunities available. If all the doors shut, that's a clear sign that I'm not to go anywhere. I wanted to go to Carlisle College pretty badly, but it wasn't in God's best interest for me. Therefore, the door was shut (even though they told me I was one of their top candidates and they *still* haven't hired anyone). Strange circumstances, but they confirm that I'm not supposed to be there.

I was taught early in discovering this process to stop here. These are the "three lights" that Fred Meyer described in his book *The Secret of Guidance.*[1] These are the three Dallas Willard uses in his book *Hearing God* (a must-read on this subject).[2] The problem with stopping here is that all three of these are subjective. I can look at all three of these and see what I want to see. When I was interviewing at White Plains, I *felt* God leading me there, Scripture wasn't in play, and my circumstances *seemed* to be pointing in that direction. I saw what I wanted to see. Now I've added a fourth piece to the puzzle. Inner promptings, Scripture, and circumstances *must* be confirmed by . . .

1. Meyer, *The Secret of Guidance*, 14–16.
2. Willard, *Hearing God*, 169–172.

4. *The Counsel of Godly Peers.* If God is truly leading me in a particular direction, he'll lead you to confirm that direction in my life. The Spirit of God is the same in you as He is in me, in my wife, in my father, in my mentors, etc. If God is leading me to a particular place, he'll confirm that through your counsel to me. Now that doesn't mean that you'll get 100% agreement on the issue. We're all different and looking at it from different angles. It does mean that in making Godly decisions and examining God's will for my life, I must consult those outside myself for their advice. For major decisions, I normally ask at least three people, and one of them will be someone with whom I know I disagree. When I was deciding where to do my doctoral studies, I asked my father, two mentors in ministry, three of the elders here, and my immediate supervisor. I knew that my supervisor and I disagreed over just about everything imaginable. I wanted his opinion, even if it was uncomfortable. He had different justifications, but his counsel was the same as everyone else I talked to: go to Colonial Seminary. The Godly Peers part of it is objective. I can't listen to your words and hear what I want to hear. I must hear what God is saying to me through you. After I got so disappointed over the White Plains interview, I went back and read my e-mails on the subject. I found that all of my peers were telling me it wasn't going to happen. I wasn't listening to them. When I was interviewed at The Lighthouse five years ago, every single one of my peers said, "This is a bad idea for you! Don't go!" So I didn't. I have no idea what would have happened, but I'm certain they saved me a lot of heartache over the past five years.

So have some conversation with Todd on how he's making his decisions. Don't unload this process on him at first. Ask him some probing questions on why he's doing these things. If he says, "Because God is leading me there," then ask him how he knows that. Keep after him. If you do, you may save him some heartache down the road, even if it's temporarily uncomfortable. If he doesn't learn to make better decisions, he'll injure himself, churches, and a number of God's people in the process.

46

❧ Involvement vs. Excellence

Micah,

Our Minister of Music came to me the other day and asked me if he should strive to involve more people or strive for excellence in the worship services. I immediately knew what his dilemma was, so I sent him to the Chairman of the Worship Committee to get his input. When asked the same question the chairman replied, "Both."

That wasn't very helpful. Our Minister of Music is up against a difficult time right now. We have traditionally been a congregation that encourages participation and service in all facets of ministry. Sooner or later we have to wrestle with the fact that not *everyone* is called to be in that particular ministry. A person may have a strong desire to participate on worship teams, but that doesn't mean that her voice is prepared for it or that the congregation is prepared to endure it. A person may have an intense longing to lead worship, but at the heart of his desire may also lie a profound inclination to be recognized for public ministry. So in all of our respective ministries we must strive to include and involve as many people as possible, but as resources those persons should be allocated to the place and time in which they will make a significant contribution to the Kingdom.

That's not always easy. I grew up in a small town where church was small, school was small, and the sports teams were small. Everybody in church got to participate. Everyone who tried out for the team, not only got to wear a uniform, but also got to play. I lettered on the football team as a sophomore because I was the only one who could long snap for the punter. I got to start for three years in high school, and my senior year started on both offense and defense. That experience profoundly shaped the way I approach team situations now, even in ministry. I want to include everyone. My inclination is to include everyone who *wants* to participate and I struggle with situations in which it would be detrimental for them to do so. "Leave no man behind" sums it up well.

I've learned over the years that you have to strive for excellence in ministry as well. God expects us to give of our best. If our best is "Kumbaya," then so be it. In your situation, that's not the best. On a personal level, if my best is perceived as an otherwise average performance, then God will honor that. If my perceived performance is not my best, God knows that also. Think of it on an organizational level also. God deserves our best. Those who are coming to Oriole Street to be introduced to Christ deserve the best. They need to know that God is not a master of mediocrity, but that he deserves all of the majesty and craft we have to offer.

How do you do it? I think you set your standards high, and you don't back down. I think you have to *model* those standards in your own life and ministry, in the way you lead your volunteers and in the way you live your life when no one is looking. I think you must do the hard things when it comes to maintaining those standards. When you set your standards high, those who don't want the extra scrutiny or effort will likely avail themselves of responsibility on your team. Say goodbye gracefully and thank them for their contribution. If they won't rise to the challenge, you're better off without them. You may, in order to maintain those standards, dismiss some people. That's always a last resort and should be done with much prayer and consultation with those to whom you are in submission. One of the worst things I ever had to do was to dismiss a volunteer. She was the wife of one of our Elders, and the potential for blowup was horrendous. The bottom line was that she'd been told time and again what her leadership team was expecting of her and she wasn't delivering it to them. It made her ministry mediocre, and because it was a public ministry, it affected the congregation. People were complaining and actually refusing to participate in this area of congregational life. It's rough, but sometimes it has to be done. Always keep in mind that dismissing a volunteer is something you do with great care, it's something you do very rarely, and it's something you do only after you've evaluated whether or not you've given that particular volunteer every opportunity to succeed.

Strive for excellence, and strive to involve as many people in that process as you can. Allocate the personnel resources as best you can. You'll fail at some points; that's a given. You'll get better at it in the long run. Every believer has a God-given gift and deserves an opportunity (and is even expected) to use that gift to advance the presence of the Kingdom on the planet. Knowing where and how to channel those gifts is a priceless resource for any congregation.

47

ஜ The Hiring Process (What to Look For)

Micah,

So you'll be leading your first Search Committee soon. Exciting! I'm excited that the Oriole Street congregation is moving to the place where you can hire more staff to help you with the ministry that's going so well there. I'm also excited that you'll be leading the Search Committee for the person with whom you'll be working so closely. I know you're frustrated about the fact that you have so much on your plate right now. The reason you're hiring this person is that your ministry responsibilities are so immense and complicated, and now you've got to see to all of those responsibilities *and* lead this search process. Gary has his own troubles and responsibilities, and you're better off having the responsibilities of this Search Committee than to have to deal with the things I see coming in *his* future.

Now to your question: "What do I look for as I'm screening candidates?" I'm glad you ask the question, for many times the only criterion for hiring a staff member in our churches is, "Who's available?" Resist the temptation to hire the first person who's available and willing to come. Since this is the first person you'll hire in a brand new ministry position, there is much at stake. The congregation is probably leery about this new position anyway and it will take a strong person to overcome their doubts and skepticism. Your reputation is also on the line as you hire this person. If it doesn't work out and this person has to be dismissed or quits, people will begin to wonder why you hired this individual in the first place. That doesn't mean that it's your fault, but you'll have to field the questions.

So with that in mind, I offer a few thoughts on how to hire and what to look for.

1. *Look for the intangibles.* As you're looking for the right person, look for the things that you can't train. Look for the character traits and qualities that don't require further development. High integrity. Strong work ethic. Commitment to personal, professional, and spiritual development. Doctrinal purity. Respect of and submission to others. Good teamwork skills. The ability to handle diversity and pressure in a graceful manner. A firm understanding of their own weaknesses. These are the kinds of things that no training in the world will help. Show me a person with these character traits, and I'll show you someone who has the personal qualities to acquire the skills necessary for any job in ministry. Conversely, Show me someone with a tremendous amount of skill in any area, but no attention to these qualities, and I'll show you someone who won't be around for more than two years. Ask yourself, "What are this person's strengths and weaknesses?" If the strengths all lie in the above character traits, you've got one to look at further.

2. *Look behind the references.* The mistake most churches make is only talking to the references listed on the resume. To be sure, you must check them. You must start there, for they are the only names you have connected with the candidate at this point. That paper is blank before it's printed and allows the candidate to put any name on it he wants. Of course he's only going to include those who will say good things about him! Dig around behind the references. When you call the reference, ask all the questions you need, but before you hang up ask, "Is there anyone else with whom this person worked closely that I might be able to talk to?" They'll likely give you a name, and you'll call that person and do the same. Now, don't waste your time. You could do this forever and not get anywhere. You'll probably keep getting the same names or the same information from different people. Get enough to confirm the candidate's history, and then move on. My own general rule of thumb is that for every reference listed I try to get three more names. So from the first reference I'll ask for three more people, and then call those (or ask for names from the second level and call *those*). Again, just get what you need. Don't settle for the reference's input alone. Look behind the references. I can't tell you how many times we've turned down a candidate because the story we got from the references was completely different

than the story we got from the people the candidate actually worked with. You don't get that information unless you do your homework.

3. *Look for someone you can get excited about.* If you can't stand before the congregation and say, "I'm *really* excited to have this person join our staff!" then you have a problem. If you can't be excited about this person, then neither will the congregation. If the congregation isn't excited about the hire, they won't participate in this new ministry endeavor, and you've doomed it from the start. Look for someone for whom you could stand before the congregation and declare your enthusiasm. It should also be someone for whom you could genuinely go to bat. Criticism will arise in any new position, and if you aren't excited enough about this person's ministry to defend them against unwarranted criticism, then you shouldn't go for it. Keep looking until you find it.

Well, that will get you started. There's more to say, but not at this time. If you have any other questions, feel free to contact me. Keep your chin up! These are exciting days for you. God is doing something profound in your life and in the ministry there at Oriole Street. Keep in touch and let me know how it's going.

48

❧ Staff for Diversity

Micah,

One thing I wanted to mention in conjunction with the hiring process that I neglected to cover in my previous post, and it's this: *Staff for diversity, not for similarity.*

Your greatest oversight (almost a temptation, but that would involve conscious thought) will be to inadvertently reject those who aren't like you. I see time and again churches in our fellowship that have a staff mainly comprised of the same persons. The Senior Minister is in charge of hiring a Youth Minister, and hires someone just like himself. The Youth Minister is then in charge of hiring a Children's Minister and hires someone exactly like himself and what you wind up with is an entire staff consisting of copies of the same person. You're an extrovert, and you'll likely be uncomfortable with someone who needs great amount of time alone to prepare for significant ministry events. You're a person for whom evangelism is a great concern. Your temptation will be to hire someone with the same evangelistic fervor, turning away anyone with strong gifts in discipleship and organizational administration. Both are needed.

When I first came to Walnut Street, the staff was pretty much all the same. In the first few years of my tenure we had a number of staff persons leave, and in replacing them we intentionally set out to hire persons who could pay attention to areas in which we were deficient. Our Associate Minister is as different from me as night is from day. I'm introverted, he's extroverted. I get counsel on life and ministry from books and from a handful of intimate friends. He gets counsel on ministry from anybody he can talk to. He likes to stand at the door and glad-hand people as they come in for the service. I like to be behind the stage praying before the service. I'm good with systems, and he's good with people. All of this we accept. Do we have differences? Sure. You can't be that different and not have some disagreements. He thinks I don't spend enough time with the people. I think he doesn't spend enough time reflecting and thinking through why he's doing what he's doing. It's like pulling on two ends of the same rope. It's only tight when there's tension.

We do agree on the essentials, though. We both have a strong work ethic. We both have a love of Christ and a commitment to the authority of the Scriptures, and we both value the input of one another. If you can create a situation like this, you'll be a stronger team. Hire someone who complements the weaknesses in your staff. If you can be open to it, your staff and the congregation will be better off in the long run.

49

❧ When You've Failed

Micah,

I enjoyed having lunch with you yesterday. I'm sorry that the state-wide program you were working on isn't going to happen. You looked so discouraged and my heart went out to you, so I wanted to encourage you a bit today.

Don't think that because this thing isn't going to happen that you're a failure. You took a risk for the Lord, and He will honor that every time. We tend to exalt risk-taking in America, but only when it yields results. God loves a risk-taker just for the sake of trying. I think he cares not for the result, but for the heart that trusts him enough to attempt it in the first place. He honors your attempts, your hard work, your diligence, and the dedication you have for Him. He even honors the responsibility that you're taking in the cancellation process, letting all the churches and registrants know that this has been cancelled, and coming to take down the advertisements quickly. These are the marks of a well-formed character and shows great responsibility and foresight on your part. It also shows that you're concerned about the image that the Lord has from Oriole Street. A lesser person would have simply said, "It's cancelled. We've put it in the church paper. Let the rest figure it out on their own." You know that people will form their opinions of Jesus based on what you do there, and you're to be commended for your integrity in that matter.

Micah, this is the time when spiritual development is at its most intense vulnerability. I know that seems like a stupid thing to say at this time. North American Christianity has taught us to believe that God is happy with us when things are going well. Sometimes that's the case. But I can say, based on my own experiences and the testimony of the spiritual masters throughout Christian history, that spiritual development is most intensive during times of seemingly insurmountable odds, pain, and cognitive and emotional dissonance. Pain and discouragement provide the opportunities and the proper emotions for our character to be revealed, and the Lord couldn't be more impressed with your character in this moment. There is still some work to be done, and this will be the formative time. (I'm not saying that God caused this event just so you could grow. That would be irresponsible.) To look this problem in the face and say, "I will still handle this difficulty with an attitude and respect worthy of Jesus" is an unbelievable testimony to your commitment and your character. Well done, Micah.

So keep your chin up! "I am neither a prophet nor the son of a prophet," but I can tell you that God couldn't be happier with you in this moment. I've heard it said that the mark of a champion is not whether he's knocked down, but whether and how he gets back up. Don't let this keep you down. Resolve now that this will *not* be the last risk you take for the Lord, and know that he's got His arm around you every step of the way.

50

❧ Saying Goodbye

Micah,

I'm sorry to hear that you'll be leaving the Oriole Street Church. Your ministry there has been fruitful, full of integrity and an enterprise worthy of mention in the Annals of the Kingdom, if there ever was or will be such a book. Your desire to leave with grace and honor is impressive also, one of many character traits the good people at Oriole Street will sorely miss. I'll offer my suggestions on leaving gracefully. I've left two churches previously—one good situation and one bad one—and I can share with you what I've learned. Some lessons you can learn from my experiences. Other's you'll have to discover on your own journey.

No doubt, some of your friends already know that you'll be leaving them soon. My experiences have always been that, while most of the congregation doesn't know about my private decisions, some of my most intimate friends in the congregation always do. They are the ones I lean on for support. They're my "Garden Friends," those who—like Peter, James, and John—would accompany their friend into the Garden of pain and help him bear it.

You'll want to inform the leadership of the congregation. If you have an Elders meeting or Board meeting this week, inform the Chairman today that you'll be announcing your resignation at that meeting.

You'll want to announce it formally as soon as possible to the congregation, preferably at the next Sunday morning worship service. The congregation has a right to know as soon as possible. Ask them to announce this at the end of the service, not during the regular announcement time before communion.

I'd recommend that the time frame between your announcement and your actual departure be somewhere between two to four weeks. Two weeks is a little short notice. You'll want to spend some time helping your volunteers prepare for your absence, and that will require some training and resource development, and it probably can't be done in two weeks. Besides, two weeks makes it seem like something's wrong and you want out as soon as possible. I'd also caution against staying longer than a month after announcing your resignation. When I left the Springfield church, I announced in April and stayed until the middle of June. It was awful. Everybody knew I was leaving so people started saying their goodbyes right away, as is natural. They were still saying their goodbyes when June rolled around and it was awkward for everybody. It was the never-ending resignation! Two to four weeks is a good time frame in which to wrap up your personal life and prepare the congregation for your absence.

Resist the urge to belittle the new Senior Minister in your departure. You may have some serious differences with him, but your volunteers and your students still have to sit and listen to him preach the Gospel. I know you can't see it now, but you and he both have similar goals, and your influence will last longer than your actual ministry. Leave a noble impression as you exit. Handle all situations with the responsibility and integrity that you're known for. Work every minute of your tenure there. Most guys check out long before they leave. Recognize that the Lord has called you to be faithful with your time there to the last minute.

The congregation will likely throw you a party or a farewell celebration, not to celebrate your leaving, but to remember you and the good things you've done during your ministry. Many of your students and your volunteers will want to publicly acknowledge the contribution you've made to their lives. Micah, this will be emotional and it will be difficult. I've never been to one of these that wasn't either. It's a good thing, and not something to run away from. Be prepared for the emotional intensity of that event. I wouldn't want to attend this gathering the night before I start my next job. Plan to take a couple of days off after this event and reflect upon the work that you've done, the lives you've touched, and the work that the Lord has done in your life since you first began there. Thank Him for every moment of it.

I'd personally recommend that you take a month off between ministry posts. Sabbaticals are not something we are commonly afforded, and you could use some serious time for detoxification of your internal issues, for relaxation, for spiritual renewal, and for anticipating the awesome opportunity that God has in store in your next post. There are a number of places you can spend (outside your family and in-laws) that are afforded free to ministers for this sort of thing. You're always welcome to come stay with us. I think you're in for some psychological and spiritual problems if you jump from one ministry to the next without time for this, and I want to help you make it happen. Don't say you can't afford to take the time off financially. I'll help you with that if you'll commit to taking the time off.

You've had a long, hard, and effective run there at Oriole Street, Micah. I couldn't be more proud of the way you've handled yourself in some of the most difficult situations ministry has to offer. You're an example to others in your field of how responsible ministry ought to be done. I wish you the best of God's blessing in your new endeavor. Keep in touch. As always, I'll be of any help I can.

❧ Bibliography

Bonhoeffer, Dietrich. *Letters and Papers from Prison.* New York: Touchstone, 1997.

Brother Lawrence. *The Practice of the Presence of God.* Gainesville, FL: Bridge-Logos Publishers, 1999. Covey, Stephen R. *The Seven Habits of Highly Effective People.* New York: Simon and Schuster Fireside, 1989.

Foster, Richard J. *Celebration of Discipline.* San Francisco: HarperCollins Publishers, Inc., 1978.

George, Thomas. "Pro Football; Lions Weigh Options and Then Plunge In." *New York Times,* April 27, 2003.

Jinkins, Michael. *Letters to Young Pastors.* Grand Rapids: William B. Eerdmans Publishing Company, 2006.

Lewis, C. S. *The Screwtape Letters.* Rev. Ed. New York: Macmillan Publishing Company, 1961.

Macchiavelli, Niccolò. *The Prince.* Trans. Angelo M. Codevilla. New Haven: Yale University Press, 1997.

Meyer, F. B. *The Secret of Guidance.* Greenville, SC: Ambassador Productions, 2000.

Mulholland, M. Robert. *Invitation to a Journey: A Road Map for Spiritual Formation.* Downers Grove: InterVarsity Press, 1993.

Nouwen, Henri. *The Genesee Diary.* New York: Image Doubleday, 1989.

Peterson, Eugene. *The Wisdom of Each Other.* Grand Rapids: Zondervan Publishing House, 1988.

Shelley, Marshall. *Well-Intentioned Dragons: Ministering to Problem People in the Church.* Minneapolis: Bethany House, 1994.

Sun Tzu. *The Art of War.* Trans. Ralph D. Sawyer. Boulder, CO: Westview Press, Inc., 1994.

Thompson, Marjorie J. *Soul Feast: An Invitation to the Christian Spiritual Life.* Louisville: Westminster John Knox Press, 2005.

Ward, Benedicta. *The Sayings of the Desert Fathers.* Kalamazoo: Cistercian Publications, 1975.

Westberg, Granger. *Good Grief.* Philadelphia: Fortress Press, 1962.

Willard, Dallas. *Hearing God: Developing a Conversational Relationship with God.* Downers Grove: InterVarsity Press, 1999.